All about the Cairn Terrier

Frontispiece Ch. Robinson Crusoe of Courtrai, owned by
Mesdames Howes and Clark, from an art crayon by Marjorie Cox.

All about the Cairn Terrier

John F. Gordon

PELHAM BOOKS

First published in Great Britain by
PELHAM BOOKS LTD

Published by the Pengiun Group
27 Wrights Lane, London W8 5TZ, England
Viking Penguin Inc., 40 West 23rd Street, New York, New York 10010, USA
Penguin Books Australia Ltd, Ringwood, Victoria, Australia
Penguin Books Ltd, 2801 John Street, Markham, Ontario, Canada L3R 1B4
Penguin Books (NZ) Ltd, 182–190 Wairau Road, Auckland 10, New Zealand

Penguin Books Ltd, Registered Offices: Harmondsworth, Middlesex, England

1988

British Library Cataloguing in Publication Data
Gordon, John F.
    All about the Cairn Terrier.
    1. Cairn Terriers
    I. Title
    636.7'55   SF429.C3

ISBN 0–7207–1786–8

Typeset by Wilmaset, Birkenhead, Wirral
Printed in Great Britain by
Butler & Tanner Ltd, Frome

Contents

Preface

It is perhaps natural that with my great and abiding interest in Terriers I have felt sufficiently drawn to the Cairn Terrier, progenitor of several Scottish varieties and himself the embodiment of the aboriginal Highland Terrier, to write a book about him. It is, in effect, a contribution, and I hope a worthy one, to those far deeper-dyed and erudite works of others we have read since the Cairn left his Gaelic twilight up to the present day. Not for me, perhaps, have been the enjoyments of exhibiting this grand little Terrier; my interests have more embraced the pleasures of owning him in conjunction with my other sporting breeds in the past and putting him to do, what for him, comes naturally – the pursuit of earthbound game quarry and other sporting exertions.

My introduction to the Cairn is a debt I owe with gratitude to my old friend, the long since departed Jimmy Garrow, a much-loved and flamboyant judge of all breeds, especially the Scottish ones. He was a master of judges in the period when dog showing was beginning to assume its vast potential. He loved the Cairn which emanated from his native homeland as indeed he loved most varieties he had encountered in his long life as a judge. He knew I travelled a bit with sporting Terriers and recommended to me my first Cairn in the mid-forties. From then on we discussed the breed on many occasions, both Cairns and their cousins whenever we met in London or around the provincial shows. Needless to say, I learned much and I have endeavoured to put before the reader a reasonably comprehensive coverage of the breed as I know it, not only its ancestry but what to do with one when you own him. He is a tough little chap, this Cairn; no trouble to keep, work and exhibit. Tough in the dictionary means strong, firm yet resilient, able to yield to force without coming apart. The Cairn is all these things – that is why you must own one because he couples these attributes with a lovable, trustworthy and jolly nature – what better recommendation could a dog have?

JFG. Romford 1987

1 Origin and History

'From the sheiling on the misty island,
  Mountains divide us and a world of seas;
Yet still our hearts are true, our hearts are Highland,
  And we in dreams behold the Hebrides.'

The origin of a breed is often obscure and the beginnings of the Cairn Terrier are no exception. Such complex matters concerning canine evolution are usually well shrouded in antiquity; it being virtually impossible to be specific in the determination of the Cairn's ancestral source.

However, it is reasonably certain that he is one of Britain's oldest Terrier breeds. From a study of art and written works, also records, it seems that the Cairn we know today differs little from the aboriginal Highland Terrier of centuries ago. When we go back into the nineteenth century, to the time when some people were starting to breed dogs in a professional manner, he and all the other broken-haired Terrier breeds in Scotland were referred to as 'Scotch' Terriers, but this was merely to distinguish them from English Terriers, most of whom were smooth-coated. It did not mean to infer that they were all Scottish Terriers, the established breed we know today.

The Cairn (that name did not crop up for the breed much before 1910) may well have an indisputable claim to an active and healthy heritage

'Terriers' from an engraving by J. Clarke after Henry Alken. Showing a group of 19th century Terriers. The three shown in the foreground are typical earth dogs of the period.

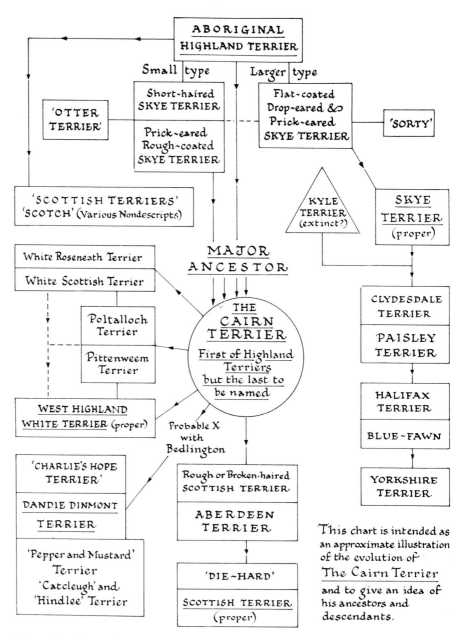

The origin of most breeds is invariably confused; the Scottish and related borderland breeds being no exception. The primitive tap-root in the Western Isles from whence sprang centuries ago the Highland Terrier and his present-day counterpart the Cairn Terrier, (the latter so named less than one century ago) indicate the consanguinity of this working stock. Most other Scottish earth Terriers and those related varieties now distributed to the Cheviots and beyond to the south of Britain should delight in claiming the Cairn as their worthy ancestor.

which stems right back into the virtually inaccessible fastnesses of Scotland's turbulent western islands. The 'winged' Island of Skye features strongly in his background, but it would appear from archaeological evidence that his existence was spread around other inhabited islands in the Hebrides. From this native primitive form of Highland Terrier, there sprang a wild and active concourse of fearless, vermin-killing Terriers. Their working platoons spread eventually to the whole of the Argyllshire coastline. From that point much later it seems, they moved on to deeper areas of the mainland, even down to the Cheviot borderlands.

There is little doubt that the breed is of an ancient lineage which can be taken back probably long before Elizabethan times. Dr Johannes Caius, physician-in-chief to the Queen in the mid-16th century and second founder of Caius (later Gonville and Caius) College, Cambridge, attempted a classification of the breeds – *De Canibus Britannicus* in 1570. Written in Latin it was translated into English by Abraham Fleming, published in 1576. The *'Terrars'* had a special section and it is conceivable that he might have had his thoughts on a dog such as the Cairn when he wrote:

'Another there is which hunteth the Foxe and the Badger
Or Greye onely, whom we call Terrars, because they crepe into the grounde,
And by that meanes make afrayde, nyppe, and byte the Foxe and the Badger
In such sorte, that eyther they teare them in peeces with theyre teeth
Beyng in the bosome of the earth, or else hayle and pull them perforce
Out of theyre lurking angles, dark dongons and close caves,
Or at the least through conceaved feare, drive them out of theyre
Hollow harbours, in so much that they are compelled to prepare speedy
Flight, and being desirous of the next refuge, are otherwise taken
And intrapped with snayres and nettes layde over holes to the same Purpose.'

These observations followed the first attempt at canine classification by Dame Juliana Berners, who wrote *Boke of St Albans*, 1486. Her treatise on hunting included the names of different breeds, with a reference to *Teroures*, an indication that Terriers (earth dogs) were categorised as being important in the working field and were in use and receiving training which would develop their natural instincts and innate skills to be passed on up the line of evolution to our present-day representatives of their breed.

As the slow-but-sure migratory period of the Highland Terrier took effect, the breed found itself in new domiciles. In these fresh homes it settled down and became established and localised. An aboriginal breed may well alter over the centuries; this change in shape, type and temperament being caused by climatic influences, by interbreeding with a dominant form of local variety or by being put to a specialised use by sportsmen and the others who owned and used it. Nature does not allow speedy changes, but consistency and persistence in breeding brings results eventually. Some of the migrants from the Highlands settled and assumed new denominations, i.e. the West Highland White Terrier, known earlier as the Poltalloch Terrier, the Scottish Terrier, with earlier names like Aberdeen Terrier and Diehard, the Clydesdale Terrier and tiny Kyle, now probably extinct. An important example, of course, is the Dandie Dinmont Terrier, epitomised by Sir Walter Scott in his *Guy Mannering*, 1814.

J. H. Walsh ('Stonehenge') said that the Dandie was a product of the Otterhound and the 'Scotch' Terrier, but it seems far more likely that the Bedlington Terrier played a prominent part in his development (See: John Gordon's *Dandie Dinmont Terrier*, 1959 and 1972). Whatever the union, the Dandie has been a 'laster', a fine yet aesthetic working variety, and to those who have owned him, a breed which carries in full measure the worth of his ancestral Highland beginnings. Similar comment must be made for our Cairn. He migrated too, but not until much later than his cousins or brothers. When he arrived on the scene he looked much the same as his ancestors appeared ages before, judging from the woodcut likenesses and drawings available for study. He had not, in effect, emancipated like the others – but he is in course of emancipating now and if his popularity in the show world, i.e. by registration figures, is anything to go by, he has marched well ahead of many other Terriers. They gave him descriptive names like Short-coated and Prick-eared Skye Terrier, albeit nomenclature which was confusing and unimpressive. Later in this book, it will be seen how he came to adopt the good and fitting name of Cairn. Much of his success can be said to be due to human sponsorship, mostly from ladies devoted to their chosen breed. Some of these will be named and recorded in later pages.

The owners of these dogs in the Western Isles valued them greatly. Many elevated them to a position well above other more mundane possessions. They admired the dog's gameness and high intelligence and assessed him for his skill in keeping down the numbers of predators who invaded the crofts and homesteads. These creatures (the islanders called them vermin) harassed the farm stock, killed poultry, even sheep and lambs, so voracious were their natures. They included the 'tod' (or fox), the otter, the weasel and badger, even the wild cat and polecat, all taking their toll of farmstock. The Cairn, as he was to be known – they called him *madadh*, Gaelic for a dog – kept these pests down to reasonable levels and at the same time served his master as a highly efficient watchdog. The local laird or big landowner kept a pack of these Terriers

A 'Scottish Terrier' from the West Highlands a century and a half ago. Dogs of this kind sometimes known as 'Short-coated Prick-eared Skye Terriers' were later to be known as Cairn Terriers. From the cauldron of their kind a variety of Scottish Terriers evolved.

on his land. The pack was used to track the outlying fox and badger to his lair and bolt the otter from his burn or hideout in the cairns, these often huge rocky ramparts, perhaps as much as a quarter mile in circumference. Such great mounds were virtually inaccessible to man, but to the Cairn with his sure-footedness and determination, they presented little difficulty. It is true that the access to some of the aisles and passages between the rocks needed careful negotiation even for such a small dog. However, the average Cairn with his intrepid nature was seldom rebuffed by such obstacles. The fox did not make his earth as one might do in deep pastoral ground. The islands were almost entirely of rock, bristly with heather and lichen coated. What soil there was did not encourage burrowing – it was too hard and solid for conventional digging – so he made his lair within the rocks where he remained well protected until the hunters arrived. The badger too was unable to form an orthodox sett and had to make similar arrangements for his security. At least, they could not dig him out as they do in some woodland areas elsewhere. It took many a dog to eject *broc* as he was known and even when this was achieved it would be after a hard-fought battle against several Terriers, most of the dogs were considerably the worse for wear, some even killed or badly mutilated by this hard-biting mammal. With such a quarry, the dogs soon learned to keep their noses at a safe distance from its vicious jaws. The animal is well-furnished with a powerful overshot mouth which bites and retracts at once. Once taken hold of flesh it seldom lets go before it has a piece of his adversary in its mouth!

The little Cairns found no difficulty in scaling the rocks. They awaited

A sporting scene on the West Coast of Scotland. From a rare 1835 engraving 'Scotch Terriers at work on a cairn in the Highlands' from a folding reproduction in Robertson's *Historical Sketches of the Scottish Terrier*, Leeds, 1900.

the leader's command '*Staigh sin!*', a call for attack which needed no repetition, so keen would they be to start the engagement. Once entered to the earth or crevice the dog would work to bolt out the occupant. Many a fierce battle would take place in the opening, very often with the Terrier lying on his side in a sorely restricted place. However, once bolted, the quarry would flee out and over the rocks and down to the coastline. There, the hunters positioned with their guns and muskets would be waiting to despatch him. Very often, the bolted animal would be dragging with him, firmly fixed to his tail or a limb, one of his tenacious combatants. At such times the hunters needed to be sure of their aim! Fox pelts, particularly, fetched a high premium in those days, the island authorities being so anxious to exterminate the vermin. They paid 3/6d a pelt – later this bounty was increased to one guinea, an almost unbelievable sum which must have seemed a veritable fortune to a hunter in such a remote land so long ago. The fox- and badger-hunters were called *brocaire* in gaelic, the word covering 'vermin-destroyers in the Highlands', and the substantial bonus for pelts kept them in great form for the job, which admittedly, was not without its hazards. Needless to say, the dogs were well looked after, for they were money-earners and fulfilled a need at the same time. Preferences for fancy points such as type, eye colour and tail carriage were very much secondary to gameness and brain, although some hunters liked a light coat colour which could be sighted easier when the dog was engaged in work.

It was not until much later in the Cairn's show debut period that fads and fancy points entered in to their dogs' lives. Special features in the

'Peto' A dog from the Highlands mid-nineteenth century. A 'Scotch' Terrier, cropped and docked. Believed a sandy-red.

dog's physical make-up, style, type and quality assumed importance to many owners and unfortunately, sometimes took precedence over character and temperament. Size, however, was always held in major esteem and so was coat quality. Size, as has already been explained made the Cairn able to enter small apertures impassable to a bigger breed, and his coat, which had to be of a harsh double texture, was required to protect him. The top coat would save him from bites and jagged projections in the rocks also from penetrating brambles; the close, dense undercoat insulated him from the wild and wet elements common enough in Skye and the islands. The Cairn's function was to bolt his quarry, not kill it – the hunters themselves saw to that with their guns. In the early days, written records show that much of this specialised form of hunting was done by three large *brocaire*. One was worked by the Macdonalds of Waternish in the north-west corner of Skye, this pack being heavily represented with dark greys and brindles; the second by the MacLeods of Drynoch, mainly silver-greys and the third by the McKinnons of Kilbride and Kyle, whose dogs ranged in coat colour from creams to some which were nearly black. The last-named maintained a historic strain of some antiquity. It was said to have been established in the 17th century by Farquar Kelly (known as Fearachar Ban) of Drumfearn, Skye, between the Lochs Eishart and na Dal. Naturally, much rivalry prevailed between the three, but such competition was useful as it aided the extermination of many vermin. Hunts used to extend all over Skye, North and South Harris and Uist and occasionally a few of the islets.

When Dr Samuel Johnson and James Boswell visited Dunvegan Castle, as guests of the MacLeods in 1773, the former reported on his stay and commented about the profusion of game in the locality, especially around the loch, and the exciting manner in which the hunts were carried out, his host using small dogs. These, of course, must have been the Highland Terriers or Cairns-to-be, although the name Cairn was not then in use. It was later, in 1887, we learn, that a Capt. W. Mackie of Port Bannatyre, noted later for his great home-bred Scottish Terrier Ch. 'Dundee', visited the Highlands collecting data on canine matters and seeking quality stock for his kennels. Apart from gleaning useful facts about the Poltalloch Terrier, forerunner of the West Highland White Terrier, he discovered the word 'Cairn' in use in certain quarters. Ash in his *Practical Dog Book*, 1930, believes that this was the first time the name had appeared in print. Mackie appears to have purchased a number of good 'Scotch' Terriers on his travels and no doubt these dogs contributed a lot to the further success of his kennels, for they would have been closely allied to the Highland Terrier to whom the name 'Scotch' Terrier was often applied in verbal and written descriptions. Also, all such Terriers were closely associated with the ancestry of the Cairn.

An indication as to how hard-bitten some of these early working Cairns were is shown in a story by J. A. MacCulloch, *The Misty Isle of Skye – Its Scenery, Its People, Its Story*, 1905. There is a reference to Captain Macdonald of Waternish's dogs, which reads: 'His otterhounds (Terriers) are famous and a dozen of them rush out to greet the visitor with shrill barks. Not one of them has a whole body, the fierce otters have deprived them of a lip, an ear, a paw, or what not, but you may be sure the offending otter did not long survive the combat'.

Probably the most informative and useful record for the student is the monograph on *Dogs of Scotland*. 1887–91, by D. J. Thomson Gray, pen-named 'Whinstone', editor of *The Scottish Fancier and Rural Gazette*, a journal published in 1887 and very rare today. Apart from the author's considerable knowledge of Terriers in Scotland he states that prior to 1879 the Scotch Terrier had not emerged from his distant and almost inaccessible Highland home. All such dogs were owned by sportsmen, foxhunters and the like, having no interest in setting their breed on an emancipation course or to develop it in any way for the benefit of dog-show interests which many despised. He makes it clear that the Highland breed was considered by some to be the modernised Scottish Terrier, whereas it was not, it was purely a 'Scotch Terrier' which was in the first place a Highland Terrier and in the second place a Cairn. Gray gives particulars of the dangers of leaving sheep unattended on the hills

A typical 'Scotch' Terrier and the Skye Terrier from Lt. Col. Charles Hamilton Smith's *Jardine's Naturalist Library*, Vol. 10, Edinburgh, 1840. This was reproduced in Ash's *Dogs: Their History and Development*, 1984.

in Skye, until the landlords and farmers in the district had clubbed together and a foxhunter was appointed. The man was paid a sum by each farmer according to the number of sheep he had to protect. The foxhunter kept a pack of small Terriers ranging from 12lb to 16lb in weight, and a couple of *luath-choin* (swift dogs) probably local staghounds or foxhounds. This man and his dogs moved about the area, and when a dead lamb was found, assumed killed by a fox, the pack was at once moved out and the culprit's scent picked up. He soon took refuge in a cairn or other hideout and the Terriers were then let loose to secure him. It seems that some of the packs used were of Roseneath Terriers, a white sub-variety of the Highland Terrier, not dissimilar to the Poltalloch and Pittenween Terriers, all so-named from the kennel or district in which they had been established. All were good varieties and respectable working Terriers. It is worthy of note that the Poltalloch Terrier was developed by Col. E. D. Malcolm of Argyllshire, but it is thought the breed suffered a deal from the hands of young and inexperienced judges. Suffice to say, Col. Malcolm allowed the name Poltalloch to be dissociated from his variety, which in due course showed as the forerunner of the West Highland White Terrier. The Roseneath breed seems to have gone rather lighter than our present day show-bench variety of Westies, although size, weight and structure would have varied.

It will be seen that with such a vast concourse of Scotch Terriers, mostly uniform in size, with a wide variety of coat colours but with dispositions and working abilities common to all, that considering the sometimes haphazard breeding liaisons which took place with outside factions in the canine world, we are fortunate in having such a standardised variety.

An insight into the work of the Cairn in his early Highland home is given in *Dogs, Their History and Development*, 1927 by E. C. Ash. He tells of a fine otter hunt one September morning. The Terriers let free went scrambling over the rocks and loose pebbles, incessantly barking, delighted. The gentlemen with their guns cocked, then arranged themselves in convenient situations for intercepting the passage of the otter, should an attempt be made to take refuge in the sea; some mounted on the tops of rocks, others stood near the water or in the boat. Of the keepers assisting the dogs to find the otter's home, one, a thick-set Highlander, addressed the dogs in Gaelic and set to with wild enthusiasm to tear away large stones from the hole. Half-burying himself to enable the dogs to come at their object: they in the meantime ran about yelping in the greatest excitement and scratching at every aperture between the stones. While this action was going on at one hole, a large otter poked his head out of another, and looked about with as much astonishment as his countenance was capable of expressing, until, catching a glimpse of one of his enemies, he suddenly retreated from the light. This incident having been observed, the attention of the party was transferred to the retreat thus betrayed. A large stone was first uplifted and hurled upon the top of the pile, with the intention of either forcing the inmate out by the shock or of breaking some of the stones. Then a pole was thrust into the crevice, which was enlarged, so as to admit a dog. One of the besiegers immediately rushed in, and after a few seconds spent in grappling with his antagonist, an otter was dragged forth, at whom the whole body of dogs ran at a tilt. His defence was the most heroic, many of his assailants exhibiting bloody evidences of the power of his bite. The battle was continued for several minutes; and to those who delight in the display of animal ferocity, the noise of enraged combatants, and the sight of wounds and death, must have afforded high enjoyment. Dogs and otter, involved in one compact group rolled down a precipitous ledge of crags, at the bottom of which, the power of numbers prevailing, the poor otter yielded up his life, dying very hard, as it is called. The otter, is in fact, a fearful opponent, and the dogs receive most terrible wounds, which, however, do not daunt their inflexible courage for a moment.

Courage in a dog is often a double-edged sword, allowing the animal to take chances liable to enter him into danger. John Lesley, Bishop of Ross, in his *Historie of Scotland from 1436 to 1561*, published in Edinburgh, 1830 referring to the Scotch Terrier, writes:

'There is also another kind of scenting dog of low height, indeed, but of bulkier body; which, creeping into subterranean burrows routs out foxes, badgers, martins and wild cats from their lurking places and dens. He, if he at any time finds the passage too narrow, opens himself a way with his feet, and that with so great labour that he frequently perishes through his own exertions.'

The breed pioneers

The name which stands out most as a dedicated pioneer of the Cairn Terrier, and about whom many laudatory words have been penned, is that of Mrs Alastair Campbell. No book on the breed would be complete without the mention of her name, and at least some note of the work she did for the Cairn's benefit in the United Kingdom, even worldwide.

Around the turn of the century Mrs Campbell was living at Tigh-an-Rudha of Ardrishaig on Loch Fyne, Argyllshire. A daughter of Sir David and Lady Monro she knew the breed in her home and became enamoured with it. She formed the 'Brocaire' kennels in Ardersier and commenced a fight for the Cairn's rights and acknowledgement in the show ring. It proved not an easy task. Two kinds of useful sporting Terriers were known in the Isle of Skye. Both had become indigenous to the Hebridean islands where they had been used for centuries to subdue the vermin which menaced the crofters' homes and the surrounding countryside. Both had, one would concede, the right to be named Skye Terriers and it was involving this point that acrimony ensued. The larger of the two varieties had been admitted to the Kennel Club registry many years previously – in effect, it had got to London first. It was a handsome breed, sinuous, glossy and very impressive and of good sporting, game temperament. Mrs Campbell's type of Skye was not quite so lovely in his appearance. He was smaller, somewhat tousled, rather foxy-looking and had up to that era, no showing experience and manners! He had been given a variety of descriptive names, 'Short-coated Prick-eared Skye' being one, the other names very similar. As soon as Mrs Campbell appeared on the show scene with her variety which she insisted should be called a Skye Terrier, uproar issued from the other side. The show ring then was not quite so rigid in its discipline as it is today – the reason for this being not so much that *all* the rules could not be enforced, but because they did not know as much about breeds and their backgrounds as they know today. Consequently, all sorts of Scotch and Skye-Terrier-like dogs used to enter the same ring. Sometimes this confused the judges; another time the lot was judged together, according to the judge's fancy!

Mrs Alastair Campbell secured a class for her beloved variety at the Inverness Show of 1908. She took along three, making her show debut with them under Theophilas Marples (Theo, of the respected *Our Dogs* publishing family). She had acquired her dogs from the noted 'Drynoch' kennels in Skye, for whom she had a high regard, convinced that they had the leading strain of the day. They had been purchased around 1905 and her three specimens were 'Roy Mohr', 'Doran Bhan' and 'MacLeod of MacLeod' – these taking 2nd, 3rd and 4th prizes with Mrs Macdonald's 'Fassie' securing the first. Florence Ross writes that the judging was done on Scottish Terrier lines, which sounds quite rational under the circumstances. Mrs Campbell's next stop was at Cruft's 1909, with author Robert Leighton judging. Some trouble started when the acknowledged Skye Terrier people saw the 'rival' variety enter the ring under the name of 'Short-haired Skyes' and proclaimed their right to the word Skye in their breed nomenclature. This argument soon reached the ears of the Kennel Club and a good deal of correspondence ensued with its inevitable acrimony. The Skye people then officially registered their protest against 'another' breed being allowed to use the name, also that they considered the particular claimant quite ineligible. Suggestions rolled in with suitable names for the little dog, the Countess of Aberdeen making a good suggestion with 'Cairn Terrier of Skye' or 'Cairn Skye Terrier' as an alternative. This was excellent and influential mediation, and the Kennel Club in their wisdom decided that the breed should henceforth be known as the Cairn Terrier, that being confirmed in 1910.

The Kennel Club received back from owners their registration cards which depicted the breed as 'Short-coated Prick-eared Skye Terriers' and issued replacements with the denomination 'Cairn Terrier'; the alteration being done free of fee, and dated from 1 January 1911. The breed was now in the Terrier Group, but for some reason – and it is assumed that because the Kennel Club had not termed them Terriers before – they had been in a section headed 'Any Other Breed of British, Colonial or Foreign Dogs not separately Classified'.

Everybody seemed to settle down happily after this fair edict from the governing body of dogs and the desire to form a breed club was soon in everybody's thoughts. Consequently, the Cairn Terrier Club was founded in 1910 following a meeting at the North British Hotel, Edinburgh. Allan Macdonald, a man who had hunted with the breed all over Skye and the nearby islets was declared president, MacLeod of MacLeod vice-president and Mrs Alastair Campbell the honorary secretary. The meeting was approved by a useful gathering of representatives from Scotland and the Western Islands. Then started the move to formulate a breed Standard; once again the North British Hotel was chosen for the meeting which was held after the Scottish Kennel Club show, 1911. By 1912 the first Challenge Certificates were put on offer at the start of the Richmond Championship Show with Mrs Alastair Campbell having acquired the rightful honour of awarding them. The winners were 'Firring Fling' and 'Firring Flora', both from Messrs. Ross & Markland's kennel. In 1913 the first champion was made with Ch. 'Tibbie of Harris' owned by Lady Sophie Scott of the 'Harris' kennel in

From a sketch by E. H. Mills, 'Jaggers' one of a pair owned in the late twenties by HRH The Prince of Wales. (*Hutchinson's Dog Encyclopaedia 1935*)

North Harris, Inverness-shire. This famous kennel's affix adorned the names of four out of the nine champions in the breed. The first dog champion at a later date was Mrs Alastair Campbell's Ch. 'Gesto'. Many great shows with Cairns have passed under the bridge since those days, the first championship show of the Cairn breed clubs being held on 14 September 1916 with Lady Sophie Scott judging at Ranelagh Club Grounds, Barnes, drawing 109 entries for the charity benefit run by the Southern Cairn Terrier Club.

Some very famous names have been owners of the Cairn, the list

An old picture of Baroness Burton with three of her Dochfour Cairns.

making impressive reading. However, it would be invidious to mention any but a few pioneers who helped to bring the breed from its lowly show-ring introduction in 1908 to its present high standing in dogdom. It is essential, nevertheless, that mention should be made of the Royal patronage enjoyed by our Cairn Terrier. The Royal Family have always been dog-lovers; H.M. Queen Victoria had a nice Cairn in 'Islay'★ which died in 1844 to her great distress. H.M. King George V had his 'Bob'. But, it is The Prince of Wales who later became the Duke of Windsor whose interest in the breed makes good reading. He was Patron of the Cairn Terrier Club from 1923–34 during which time The Baroness Burton of Dochfour was the club's president. The Baroness was responsible for many introductions of Cairns to members of the Duke's family. When the Duke made his home in France after his abdication, Mrs E. H. Drummond ('Blencathra') supplied him in 1949 with 'Thomas', a nephew of her Ch. 'Bonfire of Twobees' and others. It is said that the Duke never forgot his old dog 'Jaggers' which he acquired in the early 1920s. His first Cairn Terrier had been presented to him by Lady Sophie Scott. Others, which followed included 'Slipper' and Mr

★'Islay' featured in an original stipple and line engraving by Chas. G. Lewis *after* Edwin Landseer, R. A. entitled 'Islay, Her Majesty's Favourite Scotch Terrier, with the *Macaw, Love-birds and Spaniel Puppy*', published in 1844. Landseer's painting was in 1839. The dog was probably known as a prick-eared Skye Terrier and is called such in *Dog Life*, 1875 although from his size and appearance, particularly his head, he is a typical Cairn Terrier.

Loo'. In concluding this section on pioneers, the following names played a large part in the working for the Cairn in the early part of the century. All of them had contributed tirelessly to the one aim, which was to get the Cairn 'on the map'. They include Lady Sophie Scott ('Harris'), Lady Charles Bentinck, The Hon. Mary Hawke ('Lockyers'), Mrs Noney Fleming ('Out of the West'), Miss C. Viccars ('Mercia'), Mr & Mrs G. J. Ross ('Firring'), The Baroness Burton ('Dochfour') and a host of others, most of whom appeared in the later scene of the Cairn's evolution into the twentieth century.

Interbreeding of Cairns and West Highland White Terriers

Soon after the turn of the century, the Kennel Club permitted, even encouraged, interbreeding between closely allied breeds. Those involved were mainly from the retrieving and general gundog varieties, some thirteen such breeds being affected by the concession. Interbreeding, unlike in-breeding, entails the crossing of different yet not dissimilar varieties of the same breed, as exampled broadly perhaps, as between Cockers and Springers in the Spaniel family. In-breeding, on the other hand, involves mating closely related members of the same breed, because these are more likely to possess useful genes in common. This has always been a controversial method of breeding, not because it is a faulty one, but because it is so often applied by breeders without adequate genetic knowledge or lacking suitable stock. Interbreeding is used to produce fresh blood and in certain circumstances to reduce or increase size in a variety. Generally speaking, it is not a highly recommended process, but it does introduce fresh blood, which in the early days was required in breeds virtually incarcerated in tight, often inaccessible geographical areas.

Many early breeders had found that their dogs were showing signs of instability in general health, weakened immunity against disease, some also evincing signs of lowered procreative powers. This was blamed to a great extent on in-breeding and for this reason the Kennel Club countenanced interbreeding, agreeing in the case of Cairns and West Highland White Terriers that progeny from their resultant unions would be allowed entry to the Registry. The Kennel Club was aware, of course, that had it forbidden this form of breeding some of the more diehard fanciers would have obstinately continued with it, just the same, believing they were improving their show and working strains by the method they employed. Consequently, it was felt, officially, that rather than let interbreeding take place in a clandestine manner and remain unrecorded, it would be more prudent to leave the official Register open to the progency of the two-breed unions. Thus, white puppies from such unions became West Highland Whites and those from the darker-coated issue were named Cairn Terriers, both sorts being treated as 'pure' breeds for the purpose of the register. In 1916, some of the gundog breeders became restless, believing that the time had come for a reversion of the system. The Kennel Club was approached to repeal the system of interbreeding, reverting to 'breeding within the breed' once again. In spite of the Kennel Club's exploratory correspondence on the subject (Mr E. W. Jaquet was then secretary) interbreeding continued unabated until 1924 when the subject was again brought up and the worthiness of the system and its efficacy debated. This time, the Kennel Club decided to follow the example set by the American Kennel Club in 1922 and cease to accept applications for registration from interbred stock. On 24 November 1924 the Kennel Club, in spite of a number of dissident voices, passed the following resolution:

> 'The Committee considered the quest of interbreeding between Cairn Terriers and West Highland White Terriers, and decided that the application be refused'.

This edict took effect from 1 January 1925 and the two breeds then followed their respective paths. As we are aware, both breeds now enjoy their fine separate Standards and individualities.

A good head and expression study of a Cairn Terrier, probably one of Baroness Burton's 'Dochfour' strain.

2   The Breed Standard

The Standard of the Cairn Terrier is indispensable. It gives a word picture of what is required in the breed and is, in effect, a target at which breeders must aim to obtain perfection in their dogs. Of course, there is no such thing (as far as this writer is aware) as a perfect Cairn Terrier. There are good, even superb, specimens, but these always fall a little short of perfect.

The Standard was drawn up by an imposing panel of breed pioneers in October 1911 at a meeting held at the close of judging at the Scottish Kennel Club Show in Edinburgh's North British Hotel. A goodly number of fanciers, many of them working Terrier devotees were present. On this important occasion Allan Macdonald (Waternish) was chairman and Mrs Alastair Campbell (Hon. Secretary), Mrs F. M. Ross, Mrs N. Fleming, Lady Sophie Scott, Lady Charles Bentinck, and the Hon. Mary Hawke were also present. The original Standard survived, apart from minor additional phraseology, over the years, until 1987. Then, in common with the Standards of other breeds, a 'tidying-up' process of the sectional descriptions was authorised and implemented by the Kennel Club. So that enthusiasts new to the breed can read and compare the old with the now revised Standard, both are reproduced herewith:

Cairn Terrier Standard (up to 1987)

Characteristics This Terrier should impress with his fearless and gay disposition.

General Appearance Active, game, hardy, and 'shaggy' in appearance; strong, though compactly built. Should stand well forward on forepaws. Strong quarters, deep in ribs. Very free in movement. Coat hard enough to resist rain. Head small, but in proportion to body, a general foxy appearance is the chief characteristic of this working Terrier.

Head and Skull Skull broad in proportion; strong, but not too long or heavy jaw. A decided indentation between eyes; hair should be full on forehead. Muzzle powerful but not heavy. Very strong jaw, which should be neither undershot nor overshot.

Eyes Set wide apart; medium in size; dark hazel, rather sunk, with shaggy eyebrows.

Ears Small, pointed, well carried and erect, but not too closely set.

Mouth Large teeth. Jaw strong and level.

Neck Well set on, but not short.

Forequarters Sloping shoulder and a medium length of leg; good, but not too large bone. Forelegs should not be out at elbow. Legs must be covered with hard hair.

Body Compact, straight back; well-sprung deep ribs; strong sinews. Back medium in length and well-coupled.

Hindquarters Very strong.

Feet Forefeet, larger than hind, may be slightly turned out. Pads should be thick and strong. Thin and ferrety feet are objectionable.

Tail Short, well furnished with hair, but not feathery; carried gaily but should not turn down towards back.

Coat Very important. Must be double-coated, with profuse, hard, but not coarse, outer coat and under coat which resembles fur, and is short, soft and close. Open coats are objectionable. Head should be well furnished.

Colour Red, sandy, grey, brindled, or nearly black. Dark points such as ears and muzzle, very typical.

Weight and Size Ideal weight, 14 lb.

Faults Muzzle: undershot or overshot. Eyes: too prominent or too light. Ears: too large or round at points; they must not be heavily coated with hair. Coat: silkiness or curliness objectionable. In order to keep this breed to the best old working type, any resemblance to a Scottish Terrier will be considered objectionable.

NOTE Male animals should have two apparently normal testicles fully descended into the scrotum.

In an earlier interpretation it was included that 'a slight wave permissible' in the coat, also that a flesh or light-coloured nose most objectionable.

Further, for the guidance of *early* judges, a Scale of Points was provided, this being the custom at the time with all breeds. That for the Cairn Terrier read as follows:

Skull	5
Muzzle	10
Eyes	5
Ears	5
Body	20
Shoulders, legs and feet	20
Tail	5
General appearance (Size and Coat)	30
	100

Adjudicators found such a scale hampering and confusing as it conveyed only a series of figures based on a skeletal appreciation of an exhibit. Matters such as type, balance, proportion and soundness – all vital features in competent judging – were not allowed for. Consequently, scales of points were disposed of as being of too arbitrary a nature and modern breed standards do not include them.

All the good folk who formulated the Cairn Standard hailed mainly from the North and from Scottish areas where the initial development of the Highland Terrier (Cairn) began. They were obliged to take on and complete their task in the face of much argument and rancour from certain fanciers in their day, quite apart from many in related breeds holding a smouldering resentment to the acknowledgement of the Cairn and his emancipation as a show dog. It will be appreciated that in these very early days, there must have existed in the breed a wide diversity of types, colours and sizes. Naturally, their owners contended that theirs were the 'right' Cairns; even today some owners are perhaps inclined to consider that their geese are swans! Such dogmatists are not always easy to convince otherwise! To dampen the opinions of these objectors was to lessen their enthusiasm and possibly lose their support. In those days, with numbers few, this could not be allowed, so careful handling of the situation became the order of the day. Eventually, the Standard which was formulated became acceptable to the majority and it was passed to

Int. Ch. Divor of
Gunthorpe, owned by Mrs
C. H. Dixon (1930). (*Fall*)

the Kennel Club for approval. Exhibitors and breeders had from that
time a blueprint to work to and that was henceforth held to be the
criterion by which Cairns had to be evaluated in the show-ring.

There has existed in dogdom for many years the belief, and this refers
to many breeds, that its Standards are in certain cases too 'wordy'. Some
aver that the descriptions given in the various sections leave gaps which
are open to misinterpretation, even ambiguity. Others rightly contend
that no breed Standard can describe satisfactorily soundness, balance
and type, deficiencies in the wording which have been discussed earlier
and which of course, hold credence and validity. It is true that a written
Standard should be applied to a living specimen, which must be an
excellent Cairn, of course. Otherwise, anyone who has never seen a Cairn
Terrier could not possibly draw a satisfactory picture of one by just
reading the words of the Standard alone. This contention applies to all
other breeds, naturally, and an opinion has been held for some time that
most Standards need trimming of superfluous descriptives and the
wording made more condensed and succinct. Consequently, 1987 saw
the publication of a new official document. The following is the current
Cairn Terrier Breed Standard. It is reproduced by kind permission of the
Kennel Club (fee paid). Official copies are obtainable at the Club's
London address (*see* Appendix 2) on payment of a nominal sum.

Cairn Terrier Standard (1987)

General Appearance Agile, alert, of workmanlike, natural appearance.
Standing well forward on forepaws. Strong quarters. Deep in rib, very
free movement. Weather-resistant coat.

Characteristics Should impress as being active, game and hardy.

Temperament Fearless and gay disposition; assertive but not aggressive.

Head & Skull Head small, but in proportion to body. Skull broad; decided indentation between the eyes with a definite stop. Muzzle powerful, jaw strong but not long or heavy. Nose black. Head well furnished.

Eyes Wide apart, medium in size, dark hazel. Slightly sunk with shaggy eyebrows.

Ears Small, pointed, well carried and erect, not too closely set nor heavily coated.

Mouth Large teeth. Jaws strong with perfect, regular and complete scissor bite, i.e. upper teeth closely overlapping lower teeth and set square to the jaws.

Neck Well set on, not short.

Forequarters Sloping shoulders, medium length of leg, good but not too heavy bone. Forelegs never out at elbow. Legs covered with harsh hair.

Body Back level, medium length. Well sprung deep ribs; strong supple loin.

Hindquarters Very strong muscular thighs. Good, but not excessive, bend of stifle. Hocks well let down, inclining neither in nor out when viewed from the rear.

Feet Forefeet, larger than hind, may be slightly turned out. Pads thick and strong. Thin, narrow or spreading feet and long nails objectionable.

Tail Short, balanced, well furnished with hair but not feathery. Neither high nor low set, carried gaily but not turned down towards back.

Gait/Movement Very free-flowing stride. Forelegs reaching well forward. Hindlegs giving strong propulsion. Hocks neither too close nor too wide.

Coat Very important. Weather-resistant. Must be double-coated, with

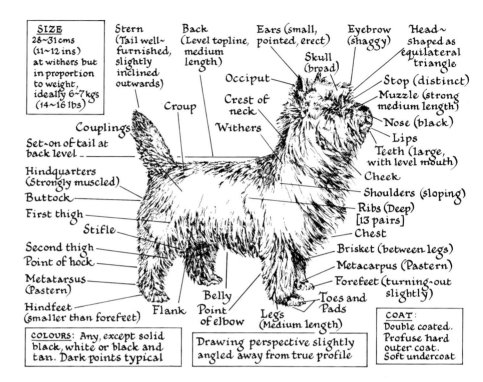

SIZE
28~31 cms
(11~12 ins)
at withers but
in proportion
to weight,
ideally 6~7 kgs
(14~16 lbs)

Stern (Tail well-furnished, slightly inclined outwards)

Back (Level topline, medium length)

Ears (small, pointed, erect)

Eyebrow (shaggy)

Head~ shaped as equilateral triangle

Skull (broad)

Occiput

Stop (distinct)

Crest of neck

Muzzle (strong medium length)

Couplings

Croup

Withers

Nose (black)

Lips

Set-on of tail at back level

Teeth (large, with level mouth)

Hindquarters (Strongly muscled)

Cheek

Shoulders (sloping)

Buttock

Ribs (Deep) [13 pairs]

First thigh

Chest

Stifle

Second thigh

Brisket (between legs)

Point of hock

Metacarpus (Pastern)

Metatarsus (Pastern)

Forefeet (turning-out slightly)

Belly

Toes and Pads

Hindfeet (smaller than forefeet)

Flank

Point of elbow

Legs (Medium length)

COLOURS: Any, except solid black, white or black and tan. Dark points typical

Drawing perspective slightly angled away from true profile

COAT: Double coated. Profuse hard outer coat. Soft undercoat

Anatomy of the Cairn Terrier

profuse, harsh, but not coarse, outer coat; undercoat short, soft and close. Open coats objectionable. Slight wave permissible.

Colour Cream, wheaten, red, grey or nearly black. Brindling in all these colours acceptable. Not solid black, or white, or black and tan. Dark points, such as ears and muzzle, very typical.

Size Approximately 28–31 cms (11–12 ins) at withers, but in proportion to weight – ideally 6–7.5 kgs (14–16 lbs).

Faults Any departure from the foregoing points should be considered a fault and the seriousness with which the fault should be regarded should be in exact proportion to its degree.

NOTE Male animals should have two apparently normal testicles fully descended into the scrotum.

© The Kennel Club 1987

Thus, it will be seen that even at best the Standard provides the outward, visible features of the dog. In effect, it tells us very little about the anatomy of the dog. So to achieve success in breeding and in judging, it is necessary to know what lies beneath the dog's skin, his skeleton, the mechanism which actuates him and how his muscles work. It is important to study every section of the description and interpret the Standard in relation to the individual dog.

Interpreting the Standard

One way to do this is to borrow the best specimen you know and read the Standard in relation to him. As you read it, savour the component parts of the dog with the relevant sections of the written description, thus:

GENERAL APPEARANCE

This is a batch of mixed virtues, all good Cairn points put together to make a pleasing picture. The dog should show a vibrant aspect, teem with breed type, which is essential to a pedigree animal if he is to represent the ideal example of his breed. His conformation should be correct and he should stand firm and present a balanced stance. To be balanced the efficient coordination of his muscles renders him a good mover, in effect, the lateral dimensions of the dog should mould pleasingly with the vertical and horizontal measurements. Equally, the head and tail should conform and contribute to the balance of the dog in outline. The Cairn Terrier, a dog built small, but on keen, athletic Terrier lines makes a well-balanced specimen when viewed in profile and can be fitted into a firm, blocky rectangle. One ponders over the word 'shaggy' in his description (see original Standard). The word is not meant to infer that the dog is clad in an untidy, tousled and uncombed coat. The metaphor is not a particularly clear one, which may account for its omission from the current Standard. Another word-portrayal which seems to have died a natural death with the advent of the 1987 Standard is the characteristic 'general foxy appearance'. Even as long ago as the mid-20s Florence Ross in her book *The Cairn Terrier*, written for *Our Dogs*, Manchester, evinced no great liking for the terminology and authors have gone to some pains to report on breed controversy which has prevailed over the years when this description has been pressed for. To the writer there seems little in the fox's facial physiognomy to justify thinking there is any real resemblance to that of the Cairn Terrier. However, the fact that the term 'foxy' came into the wording of the original Standard might suggest a fleeting impression rather than specific likeness. The length of body, lighter substance, length of muzzle, lack of stop, generous ears and distinct eye colour of the fox must surely put him well apart from those points possessed by the Cairn Terrier. Whether this is so, or not, the fact that 'foxy' is no longer an accepted term in the 1987 Standard, probably speaks for itself.

HEAD AND SKULL

The breed Standard demands that the Cairn's head should be small, but in proportion to his body. The skull itself should be broad, filled up in front of the eyes and the muzzle powerful bite, although not too long. In effect, the shape of the head should be rather similar to the form of an equilateral triangle. A too-long muzzle would give the impression of weakness in the foreface and lessen the power of bite. An important feature is the stop; this being the depression between the eyes and centrally upwards to the level of the skull. The teeth should be large and white, not undershot – when the lower incisors project beyond the upper row of incisors with a space between, nor overshot – when the upper set of incisors protrude beyond the lower set with a space between. The correct mouth is a 'scissor' or 'level' mouth where the upper set rests over and upon the lower one. Such a bite is a cutting bite and holds well. This is the formation of dentition required in the Cairn Terrier (see opposite). Bad mouths include the 'flush' mouth where the upper and lower incisors meet tip-to-tip. This form has no bite, it just nips. Also, the 'wry' mouth where the upper and lower rows of incisors cross in action. This is a mouth with little effect too. Teeth must be big and strong. The Standard demands a black nose and this section of the Standard could have well included the requirement of generous nostrils which are important in that they allow sustained and deep breathing, essential when a dog is engaged in contact with a quarry or at work below ground. The colour requirement is important for a black nose indicates that the dog has good pigmentation. It is most important that colour in a dog is dense. It can normally be checked by examining points of a dog, these being eye-rims, toe-nails, lip edges. Any sign of coloration being diluted must receive attention in one's next breeding programme. Dogs which are well-endowed with colour depth always make useful contributors to such plans.

EYES

Eye colour is important. Eyes must be dark, but not black for then they lose true Cairn expression. This is accentuated by an eye emplacement which is slightly sunken, and of deep hazel intensity. They should be medium in size and set wide apart. Any suggestion of lightness will give the dog a vapid, untypical expression. The eyes of a Cairn will tell the expert a lot about the dog's character and health and so the eyes should carry a glint and a distinct awareness. Eyes which are too small give the effect of meanness and cunning.

EARS

Correct expression is also contributed to by ears which are well-carried and of desired size. They need to be small and pointed, set on pleasingly and just off the vertical line and with some inclination to the side, but not too noticeably to the front or rear. They should be fairly thin in texture and supple. It is important that they should look tidy and be well controlled. All these features add up to a desirable expression.

The good points of the head must be complemented with a moderate distribution of shaggy eyebrows which not only protect the eyes in a working dog, but give much character and type to his appearance.

MOUTH

The essential make-up of a Cairn's dentition has been covered in other sections of this book (see p. 60). Clearly important is the true scissor bite or level mouth, which will 'bite and hold'. The count of teeth should be 42, but it is known for the incisors to lack the odd one or two in individuals. So long as it does not mean more than this, the fault is not penalised too severely, if at all. The lips should be tight and clean. The *badly* undershot and overshot mouths are normally heavily penalised, and this is necessary for such mouth formations are transmittable faults in breeding. Every conscientious breeder must strive to disperse such mouths in his plan for breeding. Too many judges see no further than

THE EARS

Correct. Set well at the angle of the skull, inclining outwards and slightly forwards.

Incorrect. Too erect and reminiscent of the Scottish Terrier.

VARIOUS MOUTHS OR BITES

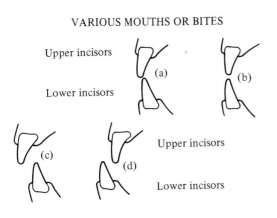

Upper incisors

Lower incisors

(a)

(b)

(c)

(d)

Upper incisors

Lower incisors

(a) The correct mouth
(b) The 'flush' mouth – not satisfactory
(c) The overshot mouth – fault
(d) The undershot mouth – fault

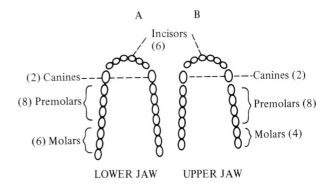

A   B

Incisors
(6)

(2) Canines —————— Canines (2)

(8) Premolars {   } Premolars (8)

(6) Molars {   } Molars (4)

LOWER JAW   UPPER JAW

A. Lower Jaw =	6 Incisors
	2 Canines
	14 Molars
	22

B. Upper Jaw =	6 Incisors
	2 Canines
	12 Molars
	20

NECKS

Correct – good stretch, not long.

'Ewe' neck. Too long, lacks strength.

Too short, lacks striking power.

the mouth of a dog, however. This does not mean that bad ones should be condoned in any way, but a judge should be able to assess the degree of misalignment in an exhibit's dentition and train himself to give a fair balance of evaluation. Clearly, in the show ring a good dog with a level mouth must beat a good dog with an undershot mouth, all other points being equal. Stock with the true Terrier mouth is vital. This type of mouth cuts and holds well; the undershot mouth can hold too, but it is not quite so foolproof in its mechanics for seizing and it is a bruising mouth of inferior worth.

NECK

This is made up of the seven vertebrae of the spine, running from the head to the beginning of the backbone. The Cairn's neck should not be too short but it should be strong, and well set on, the arch being muscular from the occiput to the point of entry at the shoulders where it will be felt to widen slightly as it moulds into the conformation of the shoulders. A good head must have a powerfully muscled neck to support it, for however typical and beautifully conformed the Cairn's head may be, its effect is nullified if the neck is weak and unable to direct its action. An overlong or 'ewe' neck lacks strength. One which is too short lacks striking power. Both extremes will militate against good balance and general appearance in a show dog specimen.

FOREQUARTERS

The Cairn should have forelegs straight and amply well boned and not short in length. The fore limbs should be of medium distance apart and set rather wider apart than the hind legs. In action the hind limbs will nevertheless follow closely in line with the forward limb movement and not be spread. The legs should be medium in length allowing for greater flexibility of action than say, the Scottie. The forelegs should be placed sufficiently apart to allow for wide and deep chest development, which in turn should be muscular and fashioned to fit into the dog's picture of perfect balance from the front, just as important as good balance when assessed from the side. There should be moderate shortness between the patella (knee-cap) and pastern (wrist) contributing thereby to good stance and balance. The Cairn's feet should turn out a little at the ground and this gives the dog an unusual natural flexibility on his feet, allowing him to move freely in all directions, pulling his body round to right, left or forward at will, an important asset to a Cairn engaged in field activities. Such a foot will maintain for the dog good balance under stress also it should be well bolstered with good pad. The Cairn's forefeet are rather larger than the hind ones. Feet which are thin, splayed and ferrety

Ch. Camcairn Claudette, owned by Messrs. Cammish & Williams. (*J. Dixon*)

are of not much use to the breed and represent a bad fault in such a highly active variety. Shoulder formation is of paramount importance too. It must be laid-back and sloping. Upright and 'proppy' shoulders are often accompanied by a shallow or concave chest. Such shoulder emplacement will make the dog's movement stilted and untypical.

Elbows which point out from the chest wall are often accompanied by loose shoulders which protrude outwards, giving a false impression of unusual width in front. Both these features are bad faults in the breed and militate against an individual's soundness. Sometimes a muscularly made dog is overloaded with muscle at the shoulders. Such shoulders were often referred to as 'bossy' in the old days and are capable of deceiving an inexperienced judge who may think the specimen power-packed in his shoulders. However, this is an inferior muscle formation to those long well-toned muscles which possess more stamina. A weak foot formation, which detracts considerably from a pleasing front is that which bears the descriptive names of 'in-toes' or 'pin-toes' i.e. with the toes turned inwards. This bad fault is often seen with elbows which

Correct, with feet turning out very slightly at pasterns, legs with ample, not heavy, bone.

Weak pasterns, feet turning out excessively; out at elbow.

Loose shoulders, revealed when a dog crosses or 'plaits' his forefeet when walking or trotting.

stand away from the chest wall, referred to as 'out-at-elbow'. All these faults are structural unsoundnesses. In a working dog, the possession of 'bossy' shoulders and elbows which stick out will endanger him in an earth where he might get stuck and make a nuisance of himself as his owner will have to grub him out and waste good working time. Reverting to the fore limbs, it should be realised that the space between them is taken up by the front end of the thorax. This contains the dog's heart and lungs enclosed by the first four pairs of ribs, lying between the dog's two shoulder blades (*scapulae*). It is of some importance therefore, that the Cairn's front should not be a tight and narrow one, reminiscent of the Fox Terrier's frontal view.

BODY

The Cairn Terrier should not be *too* short in back. One which is too short tends to be rigid and lack suppleness, an important factor in an active breed. In all cases however, the back should be powerful, commensurate with a dog of this size. It should be well reinforced with a muscular loin. The loin is that part of the body between the last ribs and the pelvis and hip-joints joined by the backbone. In the earlier Standard there was a reference to 'strong sinews' being required. Many were uncertain of its intent and the term is no longer in use, but it surely referred to the loins and limbs which certainly need to be strong in an active working earth dog. The vertebral column of the dog needs to be very flexible to allow freedom of movement and free action when engaged with a strong quarry. The current breed Standard points to the desirability of a level back of *medium* length – a short back, although favoured at one time is no longer required for it has been realised that such is a physically restrictive feature. The real factor of worth in length of back is not so much its overall length, but its lumbar formation, provided the couplings are strong and ample muscle abounds the region. If the gap which constitutes length of loins is too wide in relation to the size of the dog weakness exists and gives a very marked visual impression of weakness. It is closeness of this coupling which sets the seal of value on a medium shortish back and should it be absent the rear half of the dog will appear divorced from the front region. It is essential that the dog's make up is a compact one and one which will not preclude him from maximum agility at work.

There are other anatomical features connected with the body which make their contribution to the linkage of physical parts. A well-joined neck-to-body, also a well set-on tail, will make a back *look* shorter and a dog formed with such attributes in moderation (provided he has adequate elasticity) will be found to have a natural, easy movement.

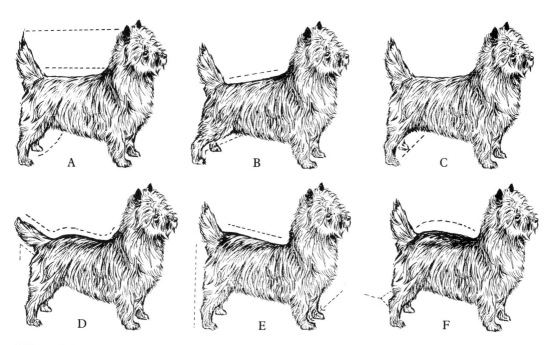

BODY OUTLINES

(A) Typical. Correct level topline; good bend of stifle; good balance. Tail position shown at ideal 11 o'clock position when viewed from left.

(B) Sloping topline; extended angulation. Indicative of general weakness rear end.

(C) Straight stifle; lacks propelling thrust.

(D) 'Sway' back, overrise at loins, falling away at croup. Tail low set-on. Due to weaknesses in local muscular development.

(E) 'Stern high'; a rising topline from withers to stern. Too high-standing at rear; ribs flat; shelly body. Weakness at pasterns. Shallow brisket.

(F) 'Roach' or 'wheel' back; spine arching upwards from withers towards tail. Not to be confused with (D). High hocks. Overloaded shoulders.

The top-line of a Cairn's back should be level as one of the Standard's requirements. Keep an eye open for the unwanted 'sway-back' evidenced by a dip behind the shoulders, due to poor rib development or spinal defect. Another bad one is the 'roach-back', shown by a convex top or back-line. It commences with an arching line from a dip at the withers along the spine to a point above the loins where the tail sets on. This abnormal arching of the spine is quite objectionable and is often accompanied by proppy shoulders. Lastly, there is the 'sloping croup'. This is usually noted in a dog whose tail is set-on too low. The croup is that part which covers the sacrum at the base of the tail and if the angulation of the sacrum and pelvis is in any case disharmonious the dog under review will move badly and be at fault.

There has been a tendency in the past for some Cairns to be shelly. The term refers to a body which is rather weakly formed, lacking rib and general substance. Much of this fault has been bred out and the average Cairn today has a firm, flexible spine positioning from the base of the neck to the commencement of the lumbar region thirteen interlocking segments having attached to them the same number of ribs. These form a sort of cage which accommodates the dog's heart and lungs. Of this complement of ribs, nine join to the sternum (breastbone), these being known as true ribs, the remaining four, not so attached known as false or floating ribs. The ribs in a working Terrier should be somewhat straight in the first few pairs, then becoming more curved and wider as they approach the rear. The ribs should be well-rounded and quite deep for a roomy rib-cage will allow ample lung room and unrestricted chest expansion during exertive working forays. One sometimes sees in show reports the term 'barrelled' applied to a dog's ribs. This is a bit of a misnomer for a barrelled shaped rib-cage is already rotund and at almost maximum expansion. It would not allow much further dilation and for this reason alone, a better term would be 'well sprung' where contraction and expansion would be possible, to the dog's greater advantage.

HINDQUARTERS

'Cowhocks' when the hocks point inwards, the hind feet turning outwards.

Correct. Firm line of hocks.

'In-toes' when the hocks point outwards, the hind feet turning inwards.

The Cairn's hindquarters should be well-muscled, the hocks well let down and the stifle noticeably bent, but not excessively so. Powerful and well-angulated hindquarters are of vast importance to the breed. The old Highland Terrier relied greatly on the strength of his hindparts to push in to earths and difficult rock crannies. The dynamic thrust of a working Cairn lies in his hindquarters and every part of this propelling machinery needs to be well-oiled and moulded into the other. Good bend of stifles, adequately reinforced with muscular second thighs, operate the hind limbs effectively and with speed from a state of angulation to one of complete extension. Only by having elasticity in his movement (and note, he cannot move as a good Cairn should, if his stifles are straight) will the dog be able to maintain his staying power. The bones which go to make up the machinery of his hindquarters must be correctly fashioned, of the right length and with the muscles well-distributed and not 'bunchy' but long and well-toned.

Other poor formations to look for include hind limbs which are set too far apart, giving a gait which is untypical. 'Cow-hocks', where the points of hocks turn inwards, coming close together, causing the hind feet to turn outwards is an unsoundness and a bad fault. 'In-toed' or 'pin-toed' behind, this being the converse fault to cow-hocks; the points of hocks

Davmar Wattagem, owned by David Winsley. (*Anne Roslin-Williams*)

turn outwards, away from each other, causing the feet to turn inwards when the dog is standing or moving. All such features militate against the overall excellence of the dog. The term 'angulation' used in relation to limbs is to describe the relationship of bones to each other in forming joints and the angles so formed. When applied to the hind limb it refers to the correct angle formed by the true lines of the haunch bone, femur and tibia. In the forelegs one would be viewing the line of shoulder bone, radius bone and humerus. Lack of angulation suggests straightness in these joints. Quite apart from the Standard of the breed, or breed points of the Cairn, it is doubtful whether any specimen lacking correct angulation could be considered truly sound. At one time, it was quite common to see straight-stifled dogs. The stifle joint is the 'knee' joint on the hind leg, and is similar to the knee in the human. 'Straight in stifle' is a term to describe the hind leg where the socket (into which the knuckle fits) is too shallow to hold the ball in place. This causes it to slip, with some pain to the dog and causing lameness. The lameness is usually only of a temporary nature, but nevertheless, is capable of losing a good dog a prize award if it occurs while he is being exhibited.

The stifle is a complicated piece of anatomy – it includes a free-moving bone, the patella (knee-cap) which is quite small and is situated in its forepart, which normally glides between the two ridges (trochlea) and a central channel at the lower end of the femur. The inner ridge should be the slightly higher of the two, and with the bone formation being normal, this would be calculated to prevent the patella slipping. However, in certain selectively bred strains, there exists a tendency for both ridges to be equal in height and for the patella to slip, when the dog may cry out and start to 'hop' with one or even both hindlegs. This often occurs with dogs which are described as being straight in stifle. It is a frequent trouble especially with breeds which have been miniaturised. The condition is not a serious one in the breed and it often repairs as a dog matures and makes stronger muscle, then it subsides, often disappearing entirely by the time the animal approaches eighteen months of age. It is stated that *patellar luxation* (patella slipping) is hereditary. Straight stifles are certainly transmittable faults and loose and slipping patellae often go with them. It is essential to avoid the use of a straight-stifled stud dog in the breeding programme, and with such care you are unlikely to produce stock afflicted with this disturbing unsoundness.

TAIL

Good and correct tails are not the easiest appendages to breed for or bad tails to breed out for that matter. The Cairn's tail in its correct form is an important feature to its owner. It would be ideal if one could state categorically the 'right' length for a tail in inches and centimetres. However, such arbitrary precision is quite impractical for dogs do vary a lot in size and contour and what might do for one would not necessarily be right for another. Suffice to say that the tail should be short and well furnished with hair. The hair must not be feathery and long beyond the tip extremity of the tail. It should be well set-on to the body, high rather than low and inclined slightly outwards at a distinct (perhaps 1 o'clock) angle and tapering to a point. Tails which are 'gay', i.e. carried very high over and above the croup, also the rather lengthy 'hound' tail which is too long and lacks essential verve, are undesirable. The ideal tail, assuming it seems to be of a pleasing length, and is set on correctly, is one which is in proportion to the size of the dog. Tail carriage normally depends upon the angle or positioning of the sacrum in relation to the spine, the sacrum finishing where the root of the tail commences. A low-set tail may indicate faulty construction in the hindquarters due to narrowness or inferior angulation. It should be noted also that tail qualities, i.e. correct length and carriage, should contribute to a desired picture as laid down by the Standard; no dog with his tail too long or too short, set on too high or too low, can be expected to express correct breed action when in exhibition. Neither will he be able to display a totally well balanced outline in the ring if his tail fails in points.

GAIT/MOVEMENT

A dog's action or movement is controlled by balance; action being the manner in which the limbs are employed to propel the dog in his particular gait. The correctly constructed Cairn will move correctly, much depending on his upbringing in and out of the kennel, and his opportunities for proper exercise and muscle development. The action of all four limbs must be positive, neither weaving, ambling, fleeting, 'paddling', 'plaiting' or high-stepping, such as seen at times in certain other breeds. The stride should be free-flowing with the forelegs reaching well into the foreground, the hindlegs showing strong propulsion and distinct drive. The moving Cairn should tread the ground neither wide nor narrow with his front feet, the limbs of the hindquarters showing some degree of parallelism when going away, the hocks well flexed and the general action an easy, rhythmic one. Stilted hind action is not uncommon in breeds other than Cairns, but our breed cannot claim immunity, let it be said, from this form of movement. It is however, a matter which has been largely righted, although examples remain to be seen in the ring. 'Plaiting', already referred to is another imperfection of gait in some small Terrier varieties; it depends on the legs being crossed when moving at the walk or in trotting. This results in an untypical rolling gait inter-paced with a short quick stride. In the Cairn, it must be remembered that obliquely laid back shoulders and well-let-down hocks are standard requirements and any specimen which is loose in shoulders, out at elbows or with upright shoulders and high hocks cannot possibly move in a typical Cairn manner.

To produce correct movement in the breed it is necessary, therefore, to fix both the structural details and pre-disposing nervous qualities genetically when arranging a breeding programme or in the normal selection of mates. Further, even a dog approaching perfection in these departments requires correct training in ring deportment and presentation if he is to express truly the action typical of his breed.

COAT

The Cairn Terrier's coat is of vital importance to him and correct coat contributes considerably to his success in the show ring. It must be a *double* coat which means the outer coat should be profuse and of hard, but not coarse texture, the undercoat being short, soft and close, not unlike fur and also very dense. Thus, there are two distinct and separate textures of coat, formed naturally for a good reason. In effect, the outer coat formed a protection for a hardy working dog, being proof against the jagged stones of the cairns, the tearing qualities of many brambles and the bites from his quarries. The undercoat, virtually unsoakable, warm and insulating to a dog whose hunting hours at night were spent largely in bitterly cold sea or river water. Open coats are objectionable says the Standard as indeed they are, and a good deal of point-making in general appearance is to be lost for the dog who owns such a coat. It is quite important to plan breeding with animals who have correct coat – a dog to bitch both with good coats almost invariably produce offspring sporting good coats – employ one of the parents with a faulty coat, and the percentage of soft or open coats in the litter may be disappointingly high.

COLOUR

It is said that no good dog can be a bad colour, but this again is entirely a working dog's owner's sentiment, where exhibiting and written breed Standards mean little. In the Cairn show ring, fanciers like to have certain exactnesses in the colour 'range' and markings favoured by their chosen breed. The 1987 Standard lists cream, wheaten, red, grey or nearly black and dark points where they fit are very typical and often desirable on ears and muzzle. The first two colours have been added to the description in the earlier Standard. It is understandable perhaps, in view of the many colours which sprang from the early recorded dogs and the sometimes dubious unions which took place, that such a wide spread of coat colours exists. It may be less understandable why more colours have been added to the recent Standard rather than reduced. However, all the colours find adherents among both pet and exhibition owners, although white Cairns are not required in view of our breed's old time association with the West Highland White Terrier when interbreeding between the two varieties was prevalent, even approved, but this is not countenanced any more. The fact that brindling in all the aforementioned colours is permissible makes the colour range even more extensive. Black (solid) as opposed to nearly black is ostracised in spite of the fact that according to a well-known Cairn lady, all blacks in Highland Terriers were purposely bred for in their island home one hundred and fifty and more years ago.

The dark points which appear on some of the colours, especially the reds, are particularly attractive and find considerable popularity with many new entrants to the breed.

SIZE/WEIGHT

When the Standard was formulated in 1911 no specific weight for the breed was laid down. However, in 1916, probably in deference to the 2-weight extension system of other breeds then longer established, weights were suggested for dog and bitch, these being 12–16 lb the dog, 11–14 lb for the bitch. Later, it was decided these weights were incompatible and a compromise of 14 lb was agreed for both sexes in 1922. Now the weight requirements read as 14–16 lb (6–7.5 kg) and the size, height measured

Ch. Courtrai John Julius, owned by the Misses Howes & Clark. (*Anne Roslin-Williams*)

from the withers to ground 11–12 in (28–31 cm) but in proportion to the weight. There still exists a variety of shapes and sizes which turn up in the show ring. These are at times, calculated to confuse even the well-versed judges and enthusiasts. However, conscientious breeding persists and fads and personal fancies will eventually fall by the wayside and bearing in mind the wide divergence of Highland Terrier types which have existed in this breed from time immemorial it is not surprising that breeders have still a lengthy path to traverse before they can settle finally for a positive and acceptable size and weight throughout the Cairn population. In today's show ring, unlike in former years, no weighing scales are to be seen. It is probably just as well – otherwise it is reasonably certain that many of the eye-pleasing winners would be found to lack weight and size conformity with the Standard! Fortunately, experienced show-goers assess such weights and dimensions with their eyes rather than resort to such impedimenta. Providing a dog is well balanced then some marginal deviation from the permitted size and weight given by the Standard, can be allowed. Slavish insistence to any detailed measurement will cramp the style of a judge and restrict his commonsense approach and interpretation of the Standard. Remember that a show dog has to be adequately covered in flesh (unlike a working dog). If your dog is a big-framed specimen, then he must be covered suitably. It serves no useful purpose to work off the extra pound to bring him within the weight requirements of the Standard. Provided the amount of flesh he is wearing is correct for his size then all you will do by reducing it is to make him look thin and probably interfere with his visual balance. It is useless to fine down (or fatten up for that matter) those which, while good specimens at their standing weight, fall on either side of the weight desired.

FAULTS

The old Standard listed faults, *viz* undershot and overshot dentition; too prominent and too light eyes; ears which are too large or round at the tips or heavily overcoated with hair; silkiness and curly coats yet while agreeing a *slight* wave; a flesh or light-coloured nose objectionable. It stated also that in order to keep the Cairn to the best old breeding type any resemblance to a Scottish Terrier was to be considered objectionable.

Today's Standard is more succinct. It says merely that any departure from the foregoing points (that is, the points contained in the Standard) should be considered faulty and the seriousness with which the fault should be regarded should be in exact proportion to its degree.

The sentence regarding an objection to any resemblance to a Scottish Terrier might raise an eyebrow as the two breeds are quite distinct. However, they were not so distinct many years ago. Crossings probably took place indiscriminately in order to produce all-whites which sold well. Those of the offspring that did not sell because of their mixed coat coloration were often palmed off as Cairns. To some this commercialised impurity gave the Cairn a bad name, all due to the influence of the Scottish Terrier, and because of this the latter breed was ostracised by specialist Cairn breeders in the development of their strains. However, let it be said the mixed coat progeny might not have been good Cairns, but they remained good Terriers for those who could use them as such.

BALANCE

This is a feature not mentioned specifically in the breed Standard, but which is essential to the Cairn Terrier himself as well as to the eye of a judge. It is the coordination of muscles, giving graceful action coupled with the overall conformation of the dog. In effect, the lateral dimensions of the dog should mould pleasingly with the horizontal and vertical measurements. Equally, the head and tail should conform and contribute to the balance of the dog's outline. The Cairn, a dog built on neat, compact lines makes a well balanced specimen when viewed from the side. When seen from any angle, the various parts of his physical make-up should fit the Standard and fuse correctly one part with the others. His action or movement is controlled by balance; action being the manner in which the limbs are employed to propel the dog in his particular gait. The Cairn has an individual style of action, treading the ground neither wide nor narrow with his forefeet, the limbs of the hind feet showing some degree of parallelism when going away with ample spring, the hocks well flexed and the general action an easy, rhythmic one. The movement has to be positive with no 'plaiting' or stilted action which might occur with a specimen which possessed an upright shoulder formation. In our breed obliquely set shoulders and well-let-down hocks are standard requirements. Any specimen which is loose in shoulders, out at elbows or with high hocks cannot possibly move properly and be in good balance. To be well balanced a dog must possess no exaggerations. His body muscles must be in complete coordination, so that seen from any angle he is of good balanced aspect, making a pleasing picture. Even his head should not be exaggerated and all the components of his make-up, his head to body, body to limbs, limbs to feet, front and hindquarters should be correctly coupled. This means that they should fuse or flow into each other, making a good and satisfactory example of his breed. A dog can be the owner of a beautiful head and body, yet these parts may seem joined together in an untidy, inconsequential manner. His front and foreparts can well be ideal, taken individually, but for some unexplained reason his feet do not appear to mould into the picture. Such dogs are inevitably unsound. It will be verified when the animal moves in any direction for there will be total lack of balance. Such animals are unsound – they should not be bred from for the tendency to lack physical integration is transmittable. Some specimens which look really good when standing and when being posed in the ring by an owner, reveal their weakness once the judge moves them, when sadly, their deficiencies become apparent.

UNSOUNDNESS

This is another serious fault which cannot properly be stated in the breed Standard without ambiguity. A dog may have excellent component parts and superb type but when he lacks orientation of these parts, as described above, he must be an unsound specimen and unwelcome for inclusion to a carefully devised breeding programme. Soundness can be inherited or acquired. A dog, following an accident may be unsound. As long as he limps because his damaged limb hurts, it can be assumed that he remains unsound. His temporary unsoundness is not thrown off until the pain stops and he stops limping. This type of unsoundness concerns us little for it cannot be passed on to the animal's progeny, being non-genetic. Soundness, like type, must be understood when interpreting the Standard, in spite of the fact that neither is mentioned. Anatomical unsoundness includes structural faults such as upright shoulders, which in a Cairn would produce stilted action and probably coarse formation of the neck and thorax. Cow-hocks, where the points of the hocks turn in to each other, are often caused by muscular weakness, the second thigh or hocks being too long. An exceptionally narrow pelvis would cause a dog to move too closely when walking away. A rear view so presented is one lacking muscular strength, the whole effect of angulation is absent and the fault is normally one of genetic origin. Being so, the effect can be dispersed only by careful breeding aimed to eradicate it. Loose elbows are another genetic fault and one certain to damn the chances and career of a prospective show or stud dog. The fault can be induced or acquired – either by rickets in puppyhood, probably due to calcium deficienies, or faulty feeding and rearing with environmental restrictions, or bad lead training. A number of other physical unsoundnesses can occur in dogs; the more obvious ones being easily recognised. However, unfortunately, some of them such as acquired deafness, and acquired, as well as inherited eyesight failings, impotency, etc, are not. These faults are normally left to the honesty and integrity of the owner (or vendor) to admit them and it speaks highly for these people that when dubious or recessive conditions have appeared in Cairn Terriers, they have not been slow in revealing the facts for the benefit of the breed.

In effect, anything which impairs the soundness of a Cairn, whether this is temporary or permanent in nature, is an unsoundness. It *can* apply to a Cairn who is below par in health and condition, working efficiency, action or character. Many things contribute to unsoundness – bad positioning while in feotal form in the dam, the effect of transient local pressure and obstructed circulation, even faulty pre-natal feeding of the dam. In puppyhood unsoundness can be caused by faulty upbringing, even too much or too little exercise or the aftermath of a contractable disease. Any breeder contemplating the use of an unsound dog should examine very closely its history of unsoundness as well as its nature. It may well be that a dog with acquired features of unsoundness could prove a useful parent, whereas one with a genetical anatomical fault is quite useless in the breeding field. Remember too, that unsoundness includes temperament and a vicious, unreliable dog, or one whose character is alien to that which is sought in the breed, can be rightly classified as unsound. Whether a dog has acquired or inherited features of unsoundness on the day of the show he has to be penalised.

CHARACTERISTICS AND TEMPERAMENT

No one who has owned a Cairn Terrier can deny the fact that this little dog has verve, intelligence, determination and courage. His character is

Lynarob Tilly Trumble, owned by Mesdames Roberts & Evans. (*Mark Mason*)

generally one of trustworthiness and stability. As in all breeds, some individuals may default in this reference, although these will almost certainly have suffered from some adverse environment in puppyhood, or other cause which may have impaired, even obliterated a desirable feature. Much has been said of these true Terrier characteristics in the past. They are essential ingredients of the Cairn and it is to be feared that there are some if not many owners who do not realise the importance of maintaining such attributes. The Cairn is not the only breed where correct temperament and character features stand in danger of dilution, even disappearance. Unfortunately, in certain strains the prized characteristic of hard-bitten gameness has gone, probably for good. This is due to the fact that those who have owned such dogs with fine tradition behind them, cared nothing for it, letting it slip through their fingers in favour of fanciers' points, many of which are superfluous and useless to the breed.

The original Cairn Terrier was a plucky, fearless sort of chap, indifferent to hardship remarkably game, smart, sharp and jolly, so wrote 'Badger' in an 1877 journal. Hard work and bad weather did not deter him. He would be ready to tackle animals much bigger, intrinsically stronger and more ferocious than himself. As a killer of vermin he was without peer, and seldom would he cry out if hurt. In the words of some of the old breeders and hunting men we can savour in full the spirit of the Cairn as he was a century and more ago in his aboriginal form. Due to these things we should consider at all times the education of our dogs, aim to preserve the Cairn spirit by working them as much as we can. Alternatively, if breeding, we should consider seriously the use of stud dogs known to possess the desired characteristics. If we ignore gameness and general toughness then as has been proved in the histories of other once courageous breeds, the Cairn will fade into gloomy obscurity. Many Cairns as puppies are prone to shyness. This to the utmost dismay of some owners who will claim at once the deficiency has been caused by in-breeding and nervousness in the strain. It is essential that patience be shown in such cases for many finely bred dogs are rather inclined this way when in early puppyhood – it is one of the ingredients in the thoroughbred which produces an ultra-keen sensitivity. Many Cairns do not show their true colours in correct balanced temperament until they are at least eighteen months old, by which time the average dog has proved that he has the very essence of what is required in a game Terrier. Sometimes a Cairn is slow to rouse, in fact, many need some provocation before setting to, but once their blood is up, they become veritable demons in attack. As young puppies they may well nurse an insult for quite a long time, and when the opportunity presents itself at a later date, they will wreak full revenge. They possess quite an excitable nature and for such small dogs can be quite pugnacious. Yet in work they are very cool and thorough, doing their job with the minimum of fuss. This characteristic makes them invaluable in the field.

For those who are interested in the working Cairn, it is as well not to enter your Terrier until he is at least one year old, although some puppies show a useful tendency to work before this age. In such cases intelligent discrimination must be used, for a young puppy can be spoilt if he gets hurt too soon in life.

It may be of interest to those interested in a working Cairn to read the recommended points for cairn-work, as given in 1876 by Capt. Macdonald of Waternish, a man who in his day, had hunted with the breed all over Skye, North and South Harris and Uist. He preferred a moderately leggy dog, enabling him to spring up boulders in a deep cairn. The coat should be thick and wiry, about $1\frac{1}{2}$ in (38 mm) long, dark brown, grey and black being good colours to own, he said. A dog should stand at $9\frac{1}{2}$ in (240 mm) a bitch proportionately smaller. The jawbone should measure 4½ in (115 mm), the skull diameter dog 12½ (320 mm) bitch 11 in (279 mm). Neck, dog 10½ in (268 mm) bitch 9½ in (240 mm). From between the eyes to root of tail, dog 22 in (560 mm) bitch 20 in (508 mm). Weight dog 16 lb (3.6 kg) bitch 12 lb (5.4 kg). Length of ear between 2½ in (65 mm) and 3 in (76 mm). Eyes, dark brown, large, expressive. Back long, legs strong, head strong, jaw longish.

The Working Terrier

As the reader will have read in the opening chapter on origin and history, the old Highland Terrier, ancestor of the Cairn Terrier, was used for sporting purposes. As his name implies (Terrier × *terrar* (Latin) = earth), this type of dog has been used from Roman times for going to ground against fox, badger and other animals who made their homes below ground level or in hideouts. It is not just going to ground which makes a dog a true working Terrier but the heart and will he has to stay with his quarry until it has been drawn and despatched. Fox Terriers have a good name for this work, of course, but there are a number of small harsh coated breeds, the Cairn among them who excel at such useful sports. The requirements of a good worker are size (about 14 lb, 6.4 kg) with a great heart (pluck and utter gameness), not forgetting brains and determination, the possession of a good nose and enough commonsense to know whether and when to make contact and give voice. The owner of such a dog must study his dog's temperament – Cairns are normally quite sensitive and abhor sharp discipline, doing more for an owner who praises and encourages. Too much pressure on a working dog will have the opposite effect to that intended.

It is not easy to acquire a ready-made worker, unless at considerable expense. However, they can be got, and provided he fits the bill by being able to prove gameness, also shows he has had experience going to ground, is the possessor of a keen nose and knowing when to give tongue, he will be worth good money. All these assets can usually be proved if he is taken on approval for a fortnight, and tried out. Assuming you make your purchase in September when the local Hunt starts its cub-hunting forays, it will be a good plan to get one of the Hunt servants to let your Terrier go to ground. At the same opportunity, you may be able to learn a lot about the game and get some useful comment on the worth of the dog. Going back a few years, the most popular sporting quarries were Fox, Badger, Otter and Rats, the last-named, of course, being well down the line in sporting class precedence. However, the modern age prohibits the hunting of Badger and Otter as both these mammals are now protected species.

RATTING

Ratting is a first-rate way of 'blooding' a novice Terrier, and getting him prepared for more formidable fur-bearing prey. The young dog should not be set against rats until he is at least six months of age, no matter what some country folk advise. A bad first-time out with a punishing rat may possibly set him back and lose him some confidence. This would be a bad thing as set-backs are not for young trainee dogs. Rats are known to carry Leptospirosis, which is usually passed on in two forms, (See: Diseases and Ailments, p. 140) usually from contact with their urine. It attacks the dog's kidneys and causes jaundice. Make sure the young Terrier has been suitably immunised before he starts a ratting career. If you can obtain an experienced ratter Terrier to show your dog how to conduct the work of ratting, the pupil will learn how to do it much quicker than you personally could achieve the training. A dog on his own and new to the work may well have no idea how to act, instead giving wild chase or running circles round the quarry. Of course, he must take hold of a rat to get the 'taste' of quarry and the game. A good puppy will kill at once, another might take two or three goes to know how he should do this. If he shows reluctance, leave him alone and he will bring his natural instincts to play and prove, hopefully, that you have made the right choice in buying him. The Cairn Terrier has a fine name for being good at ratting sport and once started, you will find he will be seeking out vermin independently and producing good sport for you in the fields and hedgerows on every country walk.

3 The Breeding Programme

Every lover of the Cairn Terrier should wish to contribute to the breed's continual improvement. Breeding dogs is a fascinating and consuming hobby – quite often it proves rewarding. The production of pure-bred dogs conforming as near as possible to the current Cairn Terrier breed Standard should be the goal of everyone who breeds from their Cairn.

Very few dog owners either understand, or, indeed, care much for genetics and certainly not many in dogs can claim a knowledge of the subject. Those who do, learn one thing quickly – that it is virtually impossible to do any more than to guess at potential from pedigree alone and conversely, just as unlikely that a Cairn's breeding possibilities can be deduced from his appearance alone. On the other hand, it must be admitted that some dogs teem with type and give the impression of latent virility, verve and power. Such as these are very often good begetters in the stockbreeding field and deserve more than a casual glance when unions are contemplated between dog and bitch.

The breeder has, in fact, only two clear factors to work with, one in appearance, the other pedigree. These two specifics, carefully calculated and intelligently analysed, will prove invaluable in an effort to improve upon his stock. Firstly, he must know how to read a pedigree. Dogs have faults (as has been said, there is no perfect specimen in the Cairn world); some of these faults being serious and transmittable, others of little consequence and easily enough bred out. However, the serious faults require a more concerted attack on them to prevent their appearance in the progeny and this is where knowledgeable pedigree reading plays its part. To know intimately each and every individual on the two pedigrees of a pair to be mated is ideal. Unfortunately, it is not always possible to obtain such specialised knowledge of the ancestry shown in these documents, although often enough a good deal of worthwhile information can be gleaned from old-timers in the breed; those whose memories can be persuaded to go back reliably down the past decades of show years. It is a wise breeder who prepares a sort of dossier on every dog and bitch, where not only their names, but also their bad and good points will be revealed and written down. This advice applies not only to a dog's physical points but to its character and propensities. To the owner of the dog in a proposed mating pair it may become apparent at once from such data why his dog lacks good ear carriage, or to the bitch's owner why his female carries her stern rather lower than the Standard edicts. He may observe faults in the pedigree that appear in duplicate, even in triplicate. One hopes that if he observes faults in the male's pedigree which reflect the faults in his bitch, he will at once dismiss the idea of bringing the pair together. Should he not heed such a warning then he would be adding multiples of such faults to the breeding of the progeny. Maybe the foregoing example is a sketchy one, but no doubt it will serve to show the principle involved by studying pedigrees and coordinating the findings to animals of good appearance when striving to produce good Cairn Terriers for the welfare and benefit of the breed.

It is more important when perfecting one's stock to observe keenly and practise care in breeding. When preparing a pedigree for study, one of at least five generations should be used. With the annotations you inscribe against each name on that pedigree you will transform the dossier into something useful and vital and revealing at once the probable breeding value of the animal studied. In effect, by examining the living Cairn Terrier you will ascertain the *visual* defects apparent in his make-up; by the study of the pedigree you will discover the latent or hidden faults he carries. These inter-related discoveries must guide you when planning your next breeding programme. Care must be taken, particularly if your research into pedigree extends back into the thirties and possibly earlier in some cases. If you are fortunate enough to have access to historic records which acquaint you with early breeding data soon after the turn of the century, you have a veritable pot of gold in your hands. However, breeding purities and reliable written pedigrees are rare, even in those dedicated days. Many of the early Cairns had common appelations; only a limited number had distinctive registration listings and it says much for the work put in by Mr and Mrs T. W. L. Caspersz in producing their *Cairn Terrier Records*, 1932 and later supplements that we are able to establish that there were 11 male lines and 50 families recorded from tail-male and tail-female ancestries respectively; these based on Bruce Lowe's oft-contested system of 'Line and Family'. This is a last century method used by Lowe of tracing a sire back to his original male ancestor, i.e. the sire's sire's sire, etc. with the dam back to her original female ancestor, i.e. the dam's dam's dam, etc. It has been noted with breeds other than Cairns that this type of recording maintains its worth and interest while the pioneer investigators (such as the Casperszs) have their hands still in the work, but it often loses much of its credence when they retire from its close study. Quite

Ch. Larchlea Here's Harvey, owned by Mrs Carole Templeton. (*Templeton*)

apart from this, it seems that very few of the male lines assert themselves from the initial listings and the families become so dissipated and mixed up that many of them disappear. So many of the Cairns from the turn of the century had either pedigrees which were not worth the paper on which they were written or were of mixed variety i.e. lacking purity and indicative of no known worthwhile ancestry. However, much of the confusion from these very early years has been well and truly blanketed with the passing of time.

Now that the history of the breed and its data are in the very capable hands of breed historian, Mrs Bunty Proudlock, we are able to look on the good dogs and bitches we know and view with confidence the intimate recording of their ancestry over many decades of good honest breeding. The eternal difficulty remains that it is not easy to find a 'dead-cert' mating pair which will produce what you are seeking. In times gone by, it was never a very simple task (unless luck played a major part) to find two good and important features going together in one Cairn Terrier. In the earlier years good Cairn heads seldom went with sound action and it often required an intensive search to locate parents who could produce progeny able to amalgamate any two desirable features. Today, with so much useful data available to breeders, the problem of point-fixing does not present so much a problem and breeders are able to give the fancy a better made and typier dog than perhaps they produced in earlier years. The standard of quality being better, the competition in the show ring becomes keener and it all gets our dog nearer perfection.

Methods of breeding

LINE-BREEDING

To line-breed, the breeder aims to obtain the desired blood and characteristics directly or indirectly by mating with the descendants of the dog whose points attract him. To achieve this successfully, he will need to select very carefully and mate dogs who have certain excellent points to related dogs who have similar good points, possibly in moderation. This would normally be expected to improve upon and fix such points. It is common to mate dogs with the same sire and different dams and vice-versa to conform to line-breeding procedure, example of such mating being:

Grandson to Grandmother		Grandfather to Granddaughter
Nephew to Aunt	Niece to Uncle	Half-brother to Sister

The breeder should take care that no such unions should be countenanced unless the pair to be mated are good specimens in themselves, show a distinct likeness to each other and, needless to say, are sound and healthy examples of the breed. With this system which, in its way is not dissimilar to in-breeding, but is much safer, one ancestor would appear twice in the previous three generations, but not within the last two. The term line-breeding is often extended to include pedigrees in which one ancestor appears twice within the last five generations. Considerable care needs to be employed when using the method so that undesirable traits (recessives) are prevented from rising to the surface and becoming fixed. These recessives will make their presence felt if given the chance and then you will get atavism or reversion to early type which is just what you have been striving against.

Once a pure strain has been established by this system, not a lot can be done to improve it while the breeder continues to use his own stock. At this stage it frequently becomes prudent to seek and introduce new blood. Herein, lies some danger, the dog to be used, needing to be thoroughly vetted as far as his effect in planned breeding is concerned. It is wiser to use a sire whose worth in the breeding field has already been clearly and irrefutably established than to employ a dog, perhaps better in written breeding and better-looking too, merely because of these attributes and economy. An untried youngster of such calibre might well ruin in no time the efforts of a breeder's lifetime. There is no difficulty in ascertaining what a stud dog has produced in his career; show results tell most of the story and the people 'in the know' in the Cairn Terrier world are often the most successful exhibitors who can recount almost any stud dog's position in breed society, which is based on the quality and success of his offspring.

No two dogs are identical, even though they are of similar gene construction. I have no intention of getting on to the science of genetics for this is a specialised field which has its own books and experts. However, those who wish to read a good book on breeding are advised to take Jean Gould's *All about Dog Breeding for Quality and Soundness* (Pelham 1978). It is apparent that as breeders become more obsessed with their subject genetics then becomes a science to read and, no doubt about it, good results come from study of this somewhat abstruse subject. When slight variations in pure lines are noted, it can sometimes be attributed to environment. Such variations are therefore acquired or non-inherited as opposed to genetic. To mention only a few such effects one can consider and muse upon fluted bone, splayed feet, loose shoulders, cow-hocks, puny shelly structure and similar weaknesses, all probably the results of poor environment and possibly ill-treatment. Such faults, as they are, are not necessarily prone to affect an animal's progeny, providing they were acquired during that animal's development and are not in its blood. The ordinary process of selection need not be affected by them. On the other hand, dogs who show the effect of undesirable mutations must be disposed of immediately for they can contribute nothing but harm to the strain you have aimed at.

IN-BREEDING

This is strictly involved with the planned mating of related dogs in order to perpetuate certain characteristics which may be desirable, and which already exist to some extent. For examples of in-breeding, one would mate together:

Father and Daughter
Mother and Son
Brother and Sister

Such a method of breeding is only for the knowledgeable and experienced breeders. It holds, as a practice, many dangers and pitfalls – for while it may well fix and cement good points, it is equally likely to do the same with bad points, some of which may well be latent (and probably unknown by the breeder) in the parents and their ancestors. Close breeding can prove responsible for infertility, cryptorchidism or monorchidism in future generations. It is useless to hope for anything but failure if in-breeding is practised with chance-bred or mediocre stock. The animals used *must* be of high general quality and free from defects in the widest sense. Unless such material is available, the breeder's efforts should be concentrated on building up a stock of sound, top-class individuals of similar type by efficient selection and line-breeding.

However, let it not be thought that in-breeding is necessarily beset with ominous overtones and can only represent a dire hazard for the breeder. Provided that the stock in use is good stock, sound, healthy and carrying within it no abnormal factors, breeding in this form can be carried on safely for many generations. There is one sure rule however, that must be followed. This is that every member of the resultant progeny which appears lacking in form, type and temperament, *must* be culled, and quite ruthlessly too. If this is not done, then in-breeding will not achieve any success, for you have to breed out the bad and mediocre and maintain *only* the good. Remember that the longer you hold on to the defects or overlook them the greater time it will take to disperse them, if indeed this proves possible without the ruination of the strain. It should be noted that the closest form of in-breeding is by putting brother and sister together; father to daughter and mother to son coming lower down the line. The whole system of in-breeding is essentially a fascinating method of stock production, but frankly, it is strictly for the experts and not really a practice for newcomers and beginners to the breed to embrace.

OUT-CROSSING

This is the mating of a pair of animals who are in no way related and have no common ancestors, as far as one is aware. The arrangement is normally made to introduce a desired feature or attribute. The system may well achieve this, but just as easily it can bring in a number of less-wanted points taken from one or both parents. Generally, out-breeding produces an uneven litter and the good points aimed at in the progeny may well not appear in the mated pairs' first generation, often becoming apparent in the second generation, i.e. the grandchildren. Too many people are of the opinion that out-crossing, i.e. the introduction of new blood into an established strain, has the magical power of improving, invigorating, even producing something sensatio-nal in that strain. This is a fallacy – not only is it impossible for an out-cross to eliminate a fault in a single generation, but even faults, hitherto unthought of, could appear. This means that any dog used as an out-cross must be genetically pure with factors capable of correcting any in-bred fault which offends in the bitch. A dog capable of imparting correction which will more or less rectify the fault is a better out-cross proposition than the stud whose bloodlines permit him to more than swallow the fault and by so doing bring to the surface in the progeny some other undesirable feature(s).

A return to an in-breeding programme is advisable after the out-cross experiment.

STOCK SELECTION

The prime aim of the novice breeder is to produce something good to prove himself in the Cairn Terrier world. It is easy enough to become deeply absorbed in dog breeding, especially if you are fortunate enough to achieve success in your early ventures in the game. First, though, it is important and essential to learn all about the breed. The Cairn Terrier Standard is the bible of the breed, which answers most questions. It has to be learned by the novice and applied by him to the living dog. Next, it is very necessary to become immersed in the breed and the only way to do this is to go to as many top shows as possible, shows where the best Cairns are on display. Watch the judging and try and follow the judge's thoughts when he places the winning exhibits. Listen to the ringsiders' remarks and try and follow their reasoning too. Sometimes ringsiders talk a lot of sense, sometimes sheer rot, for they are not close-up on the judge or the dogs in the ring and they cannot see half what the judge can. The novice must not be backward or coy in discussing the breed, its dogs, even its people with all and everyone who can help him with useful and rational comment. The top Cairn Terrier kennels should be visited and the best dogs handled and closely examined – with their owners' permission, of course. Most breeders will be only too eager to parade, even boast about their dogs and from such encounters much can be learned. However, make sure that the advice you get comes from the right people. There are people who have been in the breed a long time, but that does not make them experts, whereas there are genuine experts who have been in the breed only a comparatively short time. Learn to sort out in the circle of enthusiasts those who talk sense, knowing what they are talking about and are not patently dogmatic. Remember at all times that most people with successful dogs have had to go through the mill to get where they are; to establish a sound, healthy and successful strain will have entailed much hard work, planning, financial outlay and quite a few disappointments and heartaches. Therefore, a word of thanks and appreciation is the order of the day for any knowledge gleaned from such friends.

As you get around and mingle with the Cairn Terrier clan and inspect their dogs you will probably gradually develop and cultivate 'an eye' for a dog. This is essential, but not everyone manages to acquire this gift. A good 'eye' will save you a lot of money and help you to formulate sound decisions. It cannot be acquired in a few months, usually it comes after a year or two in the breed. Some folk need a lifetime to claim such an instinct. It will tell you what constitutes a good dog of a given type. Once you have the gift of being able to recognise the right sort, you will find it easier to pick out the right mating pair for your programme of breeding.

The old law of 'like begets like' is a sound one, although its veracity is sometimes debated. It develops from the system of appraisal normally used by successful livestock breeders when employing the breeding formula of visual appearance plus pedigree worth, already referred to. It assumes that when two parents of similar type are mated together their progeny will be of that type. Successful breeding by this method can be expected provided it is supported by efficient line-breeding. This has to be based on a clear and true picture of the parents' ancestry as far back as possible. To achieve this, the mating pairs' pedigrees have to be studied so that each and every ancestor is pictured with its good and bad points. In effect, the pedigrees have to be made eloquent with the vital facts of the respective breed histories.

To follow the system through to a satisfactory conclusion, you must find a mating pair which resembles each other structurally. They have to be good Cairn Terriers in themselves, as near to the requirements of the breed Standard as possible, and certainly free from glaring faults. They have to be completely sound anatomically and temperamentally and in first-class health. Never consider any animal with vice or similar temperamental deficiency for any breeding programme and endeavour to ensure that the female family background can claim a series of good and reliable whelpers and bitches strong in their mothering qualities. With all such favourable points present, you will stand a very good chance of producing stock which conforms to the same good type.

When the puppies are bred, it will be found that the majority inherit many of the characteristics of both sire and dam, yet there will be some youngsters in the litter who do not bear much, if any, resemblance to either parent. Thus, if both parents have excellent heads, it is reasonable to expect that most of the progeny will have good heads, but it is quite likely that a few of the members will have indifferent heads. The cause of this feature could be that the individuals affected are throw-backs to an early ancestor of whom you may not have much information. On noting the appearance of youngsters with weak heads you should be able to refer to your pedigree annotations and you might discover that the parental dam's granddam (this is only an example, please note) was commented upon for her weak head and skull. This could well mean that the dam of your puppies carries a tendency latently which she can (has indeed transmitted in this instance) in subsequent generations.

When dissimilar types of Cairns are bred together, some puppies will tend to follow one parental type and some the other with possibly one or two falling midway between the two sorts. The latter kind, even if they prove worthwhile specimens (which would be unusual), will be of little use to someone with conscientious breeding in mind, for they will pass on to their own progeny the undesirable features of their own parents. Because of this danger alone, the value of knowing a lot about your dogs' pedigrees is apparent. The more you know of their ancestry the better your chances of successful breeding, provided this knowledge is applied intelligently and coupled with the determination to succeed in the drive to produce better Cairn Terriers. This, of course, is every breeder's aim.

Choosing a bitch

In any mating pair the female is of primary importance. The commonly recognised course of inheritance, when planning a union is tail-male which considers objectively, the sire, grand-sire, the great grand-sire and so on. Because of this, the female lines are frequently overlooked and treated as being of lesser importance. This is possibly because the task of setting out a breeding programme is made easier by virtue of the fact that the male produces more offspring than the bitch, which permits the planner to assess better his worth as a sire. On the other hand, the progeny from a bitch is, of course, limited. This preference for a male's influence is unfortunate, for tail-female course of inheritance is one of the most useful and important factors in breeding true to type. Without good bitches to breed to good dogs, no real or permanent advance towards perfection can ever be achieved.

It is important that the beginner should buy the best bitch he can afford, and this does not necessarily mean the most expensive. These days, there are highly competent and reputable Cairn Terrier kennels specialising in show and breeding stock. A few discreet enquiries will quickly ascertain in which establishments the novice can place his faith and deal in confidence of receiving a square deal. It must never be thought that a bitch's conformation and points are of secondary significance. Certainly, it is necessary when breeding to select a good sire, but it is *vitally* important to have a good dam for one's puppies. Whereas with a good bitch one might breed some excellent stock with an ordinary stud dog, even the best of sires is hard put to it to produce something good out of a plain, perhaps nondescript, bitch. Good stock will never come readily from a poor specimen female. Admittedly, there have been instances of mediocre dams producing 'sports' or the occasional chancy big winner, but these exceptions are of little use to the breed generally for the poor bitch is a 'black mark' in the pedigree of any successful progeny she might conceive and which would be liable to throw back to her at a later date. Most breeders who produce what they believe to be a 'flyer' from a sub-average background frequently congratulate themselves prematurely. Such advantages usually turn out to be only temporary.

Some guidance as to how a good bitch should be bought can be given. Not many people can afford a Champion. Not every newcomer to the breed would want to, anyway. I am not at all sure it is a good thing to take a short cut to the top as then a lot of fun in the dog game can be lost. It is better to buy an adult bitch or at least a well-grown puppy as free from faults in her make-up, type and temperament as possible. Try and secure one with a pedigree which matches her good looks. Remember the quoted formula of 'appearance plus pedigree' given in earlier pages and you will know what to strive for in your selection.

Having studied the breed Standard closely and assimilated the major requirements which make a good Cairn, then study the living animal. The visual points must impress you and you will look first at the head which of course, carries the ears, eyes and consequently the expression. The skull is broad, the ears are small, pointed and carried erect on top of the skull and inclined outward a little. Untidy ears in an adult or well-grown youngster are bad features and any owner of such is best left alone. Eyes which are too close set or black are unwanted; they should be emplaced well apart, of deep, hazel colour and of medium size. Profuse eye lashing contributes to the required Cairn expression which is probably best described in the fancy as 'foxy', but do not be misled into thinking that the head itself is to be shaped like that of a fox, possibly only the expression. The gaze must be feminine, yet sharply alert, not necessarily with a piercing, gimlet eye, the prerogative of a male. Movement, both forward, hind and profile action will be easy enough to see as will angulation and balance. The forequarters are constructed cleanly, the sloping shoulder formation permitting an easy and free action. A poor gait may suggest that the feet are splayed or lacking thickness in the pads. Such deficiencies you will have to satisfy yourself about when it comes to a physical examination. Note that the forefeet turn out slightly – in a working Terrier this is quite important as it allows the dog considerable freedom of action in all directions, pulling the body round to right, left and forward at will. Such feet will also maintain for the dog good balance under stress.

Take heed of her bone; she should be possessed of ample bone, not heavy bone which leans towards coarseness, unwanted in a female. Light fluted bone is a transmittable fault and if it exists in the bitch she is unlikely to be of much use to a serious breeder. Not only will she fail to give good effect if she is shown, but her offspring will either show similar weakness or carry the fault through to their own progeny. The old adage of 'What's bred in the bone will out in the flesh', infers that what has passed down the female family line over the generations will always show itself somewhere in subsequent generations.

Deneland Girl Friday and Deneland Friday's Girl, owned by Mrs Mary Towers, hon. secty. of S.C.C.T.C. (*Kentish Times*)

Note the length of leg – if too much daylight shows beneath the body it is bound to detract from the animal's balance. Look at the length of back and the coupling, which is that part of the body between the last ribs and the hip joints joined by the backbone. At one time ultra-short backs were sought, but this was wrong for it militates against the suppleness required in an active working Terrier, thus, a 'shortish' back is better described as being of medium length. Some breeders aver that a bitch can be longer coupled than a dog. This may be true, but do not allow too much latitude in this concession, for in excess it can mean a bitch will lose points in balance and general appearance.

The tail is another feature which is contained in points for balance and general appearance. It must be short and well furnished with hair and carried cheerfully. A sickle or gay tail, i.e. carried over the croup is to be deplored and is not easy to eradicate when breeding. A too short tail gives the appearance of cloddiness, whereas an over-long tail lacks strength and detracts from a dog's good balance which is never more apparent than when viewed on a dog's rear when he is going away. Tail carriage depends largely upon the angle or position of the sacrum in relation to the spine, the sacrum finishing where the root of the tail commences. Low-set tails are bad too and are often found in dogs with a distinct falling-away at the croup. It is also very unsightly. Some of the old sporting fraternity used to believe that a dog with an over-long, low-set tail was a coward when challenged in action, but such an opinion is unlikely to hold much credence today, or likely to be proven satisfactorily for that matter.

Not much has been said about heads – the show judge's favourite feature and nevertheless a very important one too. This dominant component should carry a broad skull, with a jaw neither too long nor too heavy. There should be distinct indentation between the eyes and the distance between nose to this indentation, termed the 'stop' should be roughly equivalent to the distance from the stop to the occiput which is the bone at the top of the back of the skull. The forehead should be well furnished with hair and eyebrow, but not so much as to throw a fringe obscuring the animal's vision. The head itself should be wedge-shaped and quite powerful with its strong jaws.

Look inside the mouth. The Cairn's permanent dentition must be established with any specimen you propose to buy. Only by ensuring this will you be able to assess whether the bitch has a good mouth by which is meant not only strong white and level teeth, but with a bite which is of the correct scissor variety, i.e. with the top row of incisors resting over and upon the lower incisors with no space between. In show judging the overshot and undershot mouths are severely penalised. Some judges inflict heavy penalties on mouths which have only slight deficiencies of form and it is clearly necessary to appreciate the degree of incorrectness rather than severely penalise an otherwise excellent specimen out of hand. A badly undershot or overshot mouth is one with a visible gap or channel between the upper and lower incisors or front teeth. The Cairn has large teeth and a level mouth with scissor bite is required in work when he has to contend with vermin most of it heavier than the dog himself. Bad mouths are transmittable in breeding pedigree dogs, so you must certainly avoid purchasing a bitch with a bad mouth. One has to admit that an undershot mouth is capable of some holding power, but it is not quite so foolproof in its mechanics for laying hold or seizing. It is clearly a bruising mouth of inferior worth and must be avoided in your search for something near perfection. The 'flush' mouth where both upper and lower incisors close tip-to-tip and the 'wry' mouth, where the upper and lower incisors cross each other obliquely, are probably the two worst forms of mouth a Cairn Terrier can possess. By virtue of their formation, they have no cutting or scissor action whatsoever; further by virtue of the fact that top and bottom incisors rub and grind together, the dogs who have such mouths soon erode their teeth, which become devoid of any useful biting power.

Dogs with missing teeth, and it is not unknown for a Cairn Terrier to be lacking an incisor or molar, do occasionally miss points in the show ring. But the odd one lost is of no great concern unless it is a canine tooth which represents a useful dental armament in a sporting dog. Hindquarters need to be powerfully muscled. A Cairn needs strength behind to hold steady and push in when ground levels are precarious such as in cairns and earths. Check the bitch going away from you, watch out for such weaknesses as cow-hocks (where the hocks are bent inwards, thus throwing the hind feet outwards) and in-toes (where the hocks turn out away from each other, throwing the feet inwards). These are structural faults of a serious nature.

Lastly, and of great importance – the coat. This *must* be a harsh, profuse outer coat with an undercoat which is short, soft and close, a bit like fur. In effect, a double coat. Any indication of silkiness (like that of the Skye Terrier) or curl or indication of openness is faulty.

Colour of the coat allows a wide choice – reds, sandy, grey, grizzle, near to blacks, all being acceptable, but make sure that your bitch's colour is dense, not dilute and not showing patches of another colour. Avoid white, of course. Dark points and masks are popular and look smart. Many colours are mixed in the breed's ancestry and as the old saying goes in dogs, no good Cairn is a bad colour. However, you might as well aim to own one of a good colour!

Never be hurried into making an assessment or confirming your selection. If the owner of the bitch you are studying appears to be impatient or attempts to influence your choice with sales talk or unsolicited comment, best let the bitch go elsewhere. Any reputable kennel should understand your desire to ensure the purchase of a good bitch for your foundation; in fact, a breeder might welcome the purchaser who wants to make up his or her own mind; at least it decides where the responsibility will rest.

Given ample time then, you can assess the Cairn bitch's character and temperament. If she seemed cowed, she is no good at all, even though you may prove competent in reassuring her at a later date, for the damage has been done, usually irreparably. If she lacks verve and cheerfulness you may wish to know why. One does not necessarily want a Cairn which fusses over every stranger, but many Cairns are naturally 'matey', to use an apt expression and you can expect at least some friendliness and good nature to be expended on you. See how alert she is, how watchful, how ready for a game. Is she well endowed with true Cairn type? This is the quality which is essential to a Cairn if she is to represent or approximate to the ideal model of her breed. This is discussed in the section on the breed Standard. The possession of this attribute especially is essential to an animal required for exhibition and breeding. It is easier to recognise than it is to put in words! It is advisable to read that chapter referred to in conjunction with this.

As advised earlier, a bitch's mothering capacity is important. No one wants a dam who deserts, devours or stamps on her young. She may even carry a propensity to pass on this bad characteristic to those of her progeny who procreate in turn. A few tactful enquiries as to these points might prove useful. On the other hand, if she is a maiden, then only time will tell how she is geared and disposed to rear puppies. Should there be some doubt as to her ability at this task, then avoid her at all costs as a bad mother can prove a worry as well as an expense and disappointment.

Buying a puppy

As an alternative to purchasing an advanced specimen, you may prefer to try your hand at selecting a nice puppy of say two or three months of age. It is advisable why buying a puppy from a breeder to specify your needs, such as whether you require a Cairn Terrier for exhibition and/or breeding or merely as a pet and companion. If it should be the latter then it is reasonable to assume that the price will be lower than for a show prospect. It may well be that a pet puppy could have some clear fault or deficiency which would preclude it from winning a show competition. The reliable breeder will advise you and charge accordingly. However, make sure that you go to someone who knows how to advise you.

Let us consider the main points to look for when selecting a good Cairn Terrier puppy of say, two months. Firstly, what are you going to buy – a dog or a bitch? In the author's opinion, a bitch is often preferable. Dogs are fine if you are fortunate enough to own a good one who will evaluate himself to your advantage in the show ring. Then people with bitches will want to use him at stud and with a number of people with bitches coming to him at regular intervals he will be happy and settle down to a smug sort of existence, even developing into a bit of a 'show-off', which will make him a good watchdog in the home and an active and delightful companion on walks and field work out of doors. Such Cairns are good to own, providing you with untold pleasure. But the deprived dog, on the other hand, by virtue of his indifferent make and shape and general unattractiveness to the breeder, does not get used at stud; he can prove an embarrassment and even a nuisance. When he reaches about ten months of age and the sexual urge is upon him, he will wish to seek a mate. His natural instinct will draw him out of doors, to wander eventually well beyond the confines of your house and garden. If lost, he may become involved with police and 'rescue' bodies, resulting in much anguish being sustained on your part. Castration is sometimes considered the answer to this problem, but there is a strong prejudice against this operation. Dogs castrated as puppies do occasionally show a lack of breed character and often develop into plump, glossy and idle adults. This may be due to sterilisation taking place before the character has had a chance to develop. However, the decision in the matter is obviously one for an owner. Another unpleasant feature noted in some deprived and/or over-sexed males is a tendency to express their desires by 'working' on articles of furniture or furnishings or even upon the legs of members of the household. Such offensive manners cannot be tolerated and even with discipline applied to the animal, the pleasures of pedigree dog ownership are largely lost. On the other hand, a bitch, should she not come up to expectations in show-ring potential, may always be the medium which will allow you to breed and probably produce the show-dog you desire. She has her natural awkward times of being 'on heat' about three times every two years, but the Cairn Terrier bitch is, generally speaking, a pretty clean creature at such periods and is usually not a nuisance. There exists, of course, the hazard presented by enquiring males, but the market can offer a number of useful mating deterrents, most of them quite effective. Further, a bitch is often a better guard than a dog – her instinct is strong in guarding the 'nest'. Also, she is less inclined to wander (apart from the time when she is ripe for mating) and is probably more loyal to the family than a dog. As a 'nursemaid' to the children she scores well in points. A well-bred bitch puppy is an asset, no doubt.

When you have the opportunity of buying your puppy, take your time in making a thorough assessment and buy her between eight and twelve weeks. If from the nest, the later the better in this period, for you will then see more what you are getting. Always try and see a litter intact, i.e. before any other person has had a chance to select from it. Next, see the lot of them on the move. You will see the five or six which comprise the average complement involved running free, either in their kennel or preferably on an open lawn. From the batch, two or three will stay near you, maybe two or three will vanish, either to get away from you or satisfy some curiosity which to them has greater attraction than you. Take your time with the friendly ones; examine them on the ground while they are around your feet. Pick them up carefully one at a time – not by grabbing the puppy's forelegs and putting stress on his shoulders, but by placing a hand beneath him and cradling him upwards. Get the 'feel' of each puppy, make sure there is no pominence in the sternum (breastbone) which some might interpret as indicative of a potentially deep chest or brisket. It is not but is merely a plain case of pigeon-chest and a weak structural point. Feel the ribs; these should be well rounded and firm, allowing plenty of heart-room. Look at the limbs which should be reasonably well-boned, fairly substantial and not 'flutey', especially in the pastern (knee) region. The feet should be well formed and not spread out or splayed in the toes. A puppy's feet will usually tighten up as he grows provided he is not run continuously on soft ground. Nevertheless, the toes, even in this early stage of his life, should not show wide gaps between the digits.

Open the puppy's mouth – we have already discussed the pros and cons of canine dentition; you have in this book a diagram (p. 31) which should be referred to in this context and should clarify matters. Teeth and teeth formation have maximum importance if you are to exhibit your Cairn and enter the breeding field. A Cairn's teeth should be big, strong and white. Bad mouths existed in the breed in its early stages, or so at least we are led to understand. It is a fault which transmits fluidly in breeding and it is important to ensure that your new puppy has no leanings towards an undershot mouth formation. If the mouth is already undershot, i.e. with the lower row of incisors projecting beyond the upper set, it will almost certainly carry this fault for the rest of its life and the youngster will be of no use to you. If the mouth appears quite good, hold the puppy up and survey his jawline in profile. Some puppies, even those whose teeth are seemingly well placed indicate by their jutting and pugnacious lower jaw extremity (*repandus*) that they stand a good chance of being undershot by the time their permanent teeth have come through.

Consider then the depth of muzzle and skull. Both need to evince depth and power, even at this early age. A little shortness in the muzzle may not be a bad thing at this stage for what might appear short at say ten weeks often turns out to be of correct length at maturity. Take a look at the eyes; the darker they are the better, but sloe-black eyes are not typical in the Cairn, neither do you want a light-eyed specimen. Light eyes spoil a Cairn's expression and give a vapid outlook. The emplacement should be fairly wide in the head for broad placing usually indicates a strong head at maturity. Run both hands down from skull to muzzle, one hand on either side of the head. The feel should be one of wedge-shaped strength and firmness, and proportionate shapeliness, with ample filling in front of the eyes.

Stand the puppy sideways and view it. Although lightly built, it should look fairly square, compact and strong with a good straight back and topline, almost fitting into an imaginary square. It should look ready for action. Take its tail which should be roughly half his body length, which means it should be fairly short, strong and with ample thickness at the set-on. The bone in the tail should be strong, as it relates with the vertebrae. Take heed of the hind-legs; they should be straight. If they appear cow-hocked at eight weeks then it is clear that a lot of hard work and careful feeding is to be put in to produce straight and parallel limbs at maturity. Even then, it is unlikely that you will be able to put weak hind-limbs like this to rights.

Look closely to the puppy's front. He should have a good solid formation aft, straight well-boned legs with the elbows tucked in nicely to the side and under the body, never pointing outwards. He should have a pleasing turn of shoulder to offer. The adult Cairn Terrier's feet are allowed to turn out a little at the pasterns, but with a very young puppy of, say, eight weeks this may not yet have become apparent. If it is, then it may indicate some weakness at the pasterns which could need strengthening by exercise. There is plenty of time for a Cairn's feet to turn out a little at the pasterns when he is a few months old, so you can be a bit lenient in this point when assessing a puppy's worth. The front itself should be fairly wide – no tight Fox Terrier-type front is to be tolerated. There should be space between the forelegs for a smallish hand to be placed on the chest under the brisket. It should feel reasonably muscular, quite deep and solid. Put the puppy down and let it cavort around. Small puppies are often difficult to assess in action as they will leap and climb and twist, so get the breeder to call it away from you. He will run in a straight line, more or less. Get behind it and you will note any obvious imperfections in his action. Contrive then to have him run at you so that you can assess his forward action and physical soundness.

Pick him up again, turn him over and examine his genitals. At eight weeks it is not always possible to determine whether a male is entire, i.e. with both testicles descended into the scrotum. However, it may be obvious and if assured on this point, then all is well. If it cannot be determined then you take a chance if you accept the puppy. However, in about eight cases out of ten your chances are that he will prove eventually to be entire. Ears are difficult to assess in young puppies fresh from the nest. Sometimes, tiny, thin tissue ears with thickish cartilage where they set on the skull, turn out semi-erect, but mainly they prove to reach erectness with complete dentition or when matured which is what is required in your Cairn. Sometimes, a soft or semi-erect ear is encountered – such as these should be a warning to the buyer for they seldom shape up correctly, later. However, ears are not really a major problem with the breed these days so it is not too much of a worry for the new buyer. It is a good idea, if the sire and dam are around to have a look at their ears for ear-type is transmitted freely and if, on examination, you approve a puppy's ears and later satisfy yourself as to the parents' ears, then you are usually on quite safe ground.

The small puppy's coat prospects are seldom easy to assess without experience in the selection of youngsters for show and breeding. It is of vital importance in a Cairn to have a dense, hard coat. A soft coat can never be brought round to any semblance of harshness, but it has been found that a dog (and this applies to many breeds) kennelled in dry, fairly spartan conditions can be improved in coat texture. However, if you ever acquire a soft-coated Cairn, it is best to find him a home elsewhere, as he will not contribute well in any serious breeding programme or in exhibition. Lastly, ensure that you pick a puppy with verve and fire – don't be misled by a puppy which dashes around in a stupid, break-neck fashion. Try and find a lively, seemingly intelligent one with a bold, natural manner. Avoid at all costs one which skulks away from you and the rest of his fellows or one which shies furtively away from your outstretched hand. These are often the symptoms of unreliability.

A smart Cairn Terrier puppy. (*Anne Roslin-Williams*)

It goes without saying that if you note any undue redness or rashes, spots etc, that you will query these with the breeder; the same applying to a bump on the navel. This is probably an umbilical hernia – in effect, a rupture. Actually, it sounds worse than it is, assuming it is a small one. They often occur with first-borns out of a maiden bitch, who has been agitated or anxious in producing her first puppy at her initial whelping. These bumps are unsightly, but not usually considered an unsoundness. It is better to buy a puppy without one, but if you do succumb then your veterinary surgeon can deal with the hernia quite simply.

Check for infestation – even the best run kennels sometimes find themselves plagued with parasites brought in with natural bedding. Lift up and look under the puppy's tail and run a finger downwards against the coat from tail to neck along the spine. Any mites resident will soon reveal themselves.

The foregoing factors apply, as has been said, to selecting a puppy of around eight to twelve weeks of age. For the person who is anxious to strengthen his chances of owning a show specimen, then his choice must be from older, more mature puppies. There are experts (*sic*) who aver that they can pick a champion from a newborn litter, but these need a lot of luck on their side. The best chances of success come usually from five-month old youngsters – if you can find a beauty then your chances of owning a winner are good. The only thing is, that such a puppy will probably prove expensive for his new owner to buy; if the breeder knows a good Cairn, he will probably have a good idea of its market value. On the other hand, many experienced breeders have been known to run on for several weeks a couple of very promising youngsters from their litter in an effort to hit the jackpot with one of them, only to sell the 'flyer' from the pair and retain the mediocre one for themselves by mistake! Be sure that before you take your puppy home you collect his documents and also a feeding chart of some description to inform you of the type of feeding he has been used to. If you travel home by car, a companion who will nurse the puppy on his or her own warm lap will be less frightening to it. This is better than putting it into a small dark box and inflicting a bumpy journey on the back seat for him all the way home.

Choosing the sire

It should not be thought that the wins attributed to a stud dog necessarily make him a good sire. A lot of breeders are influenced by a dog's show wins which may well not be of much value when properly assessed. It is not unusual for a dog to win his title in quite mediocre competition or at shows which are unpopular with exhibitors and are sparsely attended. Such shows could be located in inconvenient geographical venues or rendered unpalatable to an exhibitor owing to a bad classification or promotion. It may be that the person adjudicating is not popular – some judges are not. For such reasons it is important to the bitch owner who seeks a stud for his charge to attend as many big shows as he can. There he should find the best of Cairns doing the show circuit in the current year and feast his eyes upon them. He might then be able to assess the worth of every win for himself.

A stud dog should be chosen solely for the value of his progeny rather than for the number of prizes he has won personally. It is only by employing the former rule that you will become a successful breeder. You may have a great bitch, but she will have some fault, of that you can be sure; the perfect one has yet to be born and it is essential for your own well-advised to give up the idea of pedigree dog breeding forthwith. Only a man who knows the faults and weaknesses in his particular Cairn can have any hope of correcting them. It is possible to breed out any deficiency with care and calculation over a number of generations, according to the intensity of that fault and the time available. However, the planning to achieve the eradication of unwanted features without introducing new faults, i.e. those hitherto non-existent, is the work of a dedicated breeder.

Some misinformed breeders think the way to correct a fault is to utilise a stud dog endowed with the exact opposite of that fault. For example, suppose your bitch is too high on the leg, the mistaken theory is that she should be mated to a dog who is too low to ground, expecting that one extreme will effectively cancel out the other. In fact, that is putting fault to fault and accentuating them, no less! It is feasible, of course, that an odd puppy or two will crop up falling midway between the two fault- holding parental types, but the resultant litter would contain some puppies which were too high on the leg (resembling their dam) and some which were too low to ground (resembling their sire). Worst of all, the whole litter, however it finished up individually, would represent indifferent breeding potential when the time came round for them to reproduce, for they would carry the tendency to transmit both parents' inherent faults to their progeny. The secret in breeding is to find a stud dog for the exampled bitch who is the correct height, then, as has been shown, some puppies would tend to be correct in their height – not only that, but they would carry the power to transmit only one fault – i.e. their dam's legginess, rather than two faults, legginess and shortness. It will be realised that this illustrates only one example, but numerous examples can be made by applying any pair of opposite faulty characteristics, for instance apple heads and narrow skulls, loose shoulders and Fox Terrier fronts and so on.

Mating

It is unwise to mate a bitch at her first heat, normally expected to occur when a young Cairn bitch is about eight months old, although her *oestrum* or heat or season can start a month or two earlier than this, clearly too soon to think about letting her have a family, for it is rather unfair to burden her thus. Some breeders argue that she would get mated in the wild at first heat, but then our average Cairn bitch is not conditioned to the wild. Apart from this there is also a chance that a young bitch would 'miss' or worse, get involved with whelping complications which could ruin her for good. This might apply especially in the case of an immature specimen. Most breeders favour the second heat for first-time mating and this principle would normally point to breeding with a bitch of say, fourteen months of age. By this time she would have reached a ripe yearling stage and be able to embrace the sometimes onerous duties of motherhood in her stride. Thereafter, it is prudent to let her leapfrog her next heat and be mated again at her third time round. This is a typical staggered pattern applied by many breeders of experience, but watch must be kept always on a bitch's health, strength and body development to ensure that she is mated only when she is apparently fit enough to cope with puppies.

When planning a mating and having decided which stud dog to use with the bitch, a provisional booking should be made with his owner. This advice can be confirmed as soon as the bitch begins to show 'colour' when a definite date, about twelve days ahead, can be determined. As is commonly known, a bitch's period of season or heat (or *oestrum*) is between sixteen and twenty-one days. It is first noted when the vulva begins to swell, this being followed by a discharge of mucous substance which later becomes tinged with blood. No definite time can be given for mating a bitch, as individuals vary, often quite considerably. The best time, usually, is when the coloured discharge from the vagina subsides for a day or two. Some bitches will be found ready to receive a dog at any time between the tenth and fifteenth day, but others have to be 'caught' at a certain time, often experiencing just a few hours of ripeness around the middle of their season. If the bitch is this way disposed, then special arrangements will need to be made. The best plan is to kennel her near to the selected stud dog during her vital period so that she can be introduced to him as soon as she shows willing. Frankly, such bitches are a nuisance, but if she is a good one and the chances of producing something good from her exist, then it can be worth devoting a little extra expense and trouble to the situation. Most bitches are ready for union on their twelfth or thirteenth day.

It is normal procedure to take the bitch to the dog. If the stud dog resides a long way off, then you may have to travel the bitch to him by rail or car. It is best to take her there yourself. By so doing you save her consternation and distress at a time which is critical to her and not only that, you can preside at the mating and be sure that the union is a success with the stud dog of your choice. Further the bitch is far more likely to conduct herself willingly at the mating if you are standing by her. Bitches bustled alone into an unknown house or kennel with strange humans and a bombastic stud dog become unhappy and often prove uncooperative. They frequently 'miss' because of these upsets and then all the time and expense entailed has been wasted and there is another six months to go before you can try her again.

The best time for mating is early morning, both dog and bitch having had ample opportunity to run around first and empty themselves prior to the union. Neither animal should have been fed for at least twelve hours previously. If your bitch is a maiden and the stud dog you have chosen for her is experienced, then everything will probably go well for the dog will probably conduct matters efficiently.

However, if the dog is an untried one, some care will have to be taken. He will probably rush around all over the place in excited anticipation, act stupidly and put the bitch so ill at ease that she will either attack her suitor or refuse completely to cooperate with him even when finally he calms down. With the possibility of such a disorderly mating it is advisable to have present a helper with some experience of matings.

The bitch's owner should hold her collar firmly and the best way to do this is to put the thumbs under her collar and hold her in place firmly, so that her head is steadied. It has been known that some breeders use a tape or muzzle if the bitch is a difficult one, but this is somewhat drastic and should be quite unnecessary, anything which savours of a forced mating should be considered strictly taboo. Assuming that the bitch is accepting the dog with good grace, there may be nothing much for the handlers to do. However, if difficulties occur, it may become necessary to uplift the bitch's loins to aid the dog's entry. Some dogs require a little manipulation to get them going and some contrived guidance into the bitch's vulva, a handler's aid and cooperation is appreciated by the trained stud dog. The author had a Terrier dog so well trained (or so well disposed) that he refused to do anything except the sexual act itself! The bitch would arrive and stand there ready or recalcitrant, as the mood took her, expecting him to rush her, which he did not. Instead, he would glance idly at her, look up at his handler and wait for the bitch to be placed rear end towards him. He would then mount her at once and the whole thing would be over in no time. He had well over a hundred matings, hardly any of which were 'misses' and these were usually attributed to the bitches!

A 'natural' mating is recommended by many breeders. This entails leaving both stud dog and bitch in season to their own devices. It is hoped that they will effect copulation without any outside assistance. This is all very well if it works out satisfactorily, but it does occur that such matings are occasioned with either one or both of the animals suffering some distress. Always supervise a mating. Pedigree Cairn Terriers have a high monetary value these days and tough though they may be, there seems little sense in leaving two small, but sturdy and strong-willed dogs alone in a run or paddock and returning later to find slit ears, gashed eyes, or at worst, a ruptured stud dog. Calamities like this can occur even between a pair who normally run amicably together.

The dog's natural instinct will cause him to take the initiative in the mating and once he has entered the bitch, his owner may prefer to hold him there for a few moments, both animals being 'steadied' until a 'tie' has been effected. This will indicate conclusively that seminal fluid is being deposited. The 'tie', although not essential, is always a very satisfactory state to witness when mating dogs; it lasts usually between fifteen and thirty minutes. During this time the two animals will probably have brought themselves round tail-to-tail, the accepted position for mating dogs. Should they seem to be struggling to get round to achieve this formation, the handlers should assist them. One should hold the bitch's head, the other gently swivel the male round, lifting one of his hind legs up and over the bitch's back. Keep on swivelling his head round and the lifted leg will follow round too and eventually come down to the ground. Both animals will then be perfectly comfortable and can be left so placed. So that the bitch should not march forward dragging the dog backwards behind her while the union is taking effect, the pair are best watched until the dog disengages. He should then be removed from her presence and left in a quiet room or abode to regain his composure. His personal comfort can be attended to, if necessary, by ensuring that the sheath covering the penis has been returned to its natural position. Both animals should be watered and rested after adequate feeding. One service is usually sufficient from a dog regularly at stud. An untried dog, having his first successful mating could be allowed another with the same bitch within

Ch. Brockis of Benliath, owned by Miss Jessie Wood. (*Anne Roslin-Williams*)

thirty-six hours of the first, if one's convenience allows. It may be that the first service will have done nothing but stimulate the second, hence this precaution.

Some explanation as to the workings of a 'tie' might be in order in this section. It occurs when a dog has entered a bitch to the extent of his final thrust and is pumping something like several million sperm into her. At this stage his penis will have undergone some change. It will have swollen to three or four times its normal size and the bulb, which is rather a hard swelling, the size and shape of a small sphere, situated half way along the length of the penis, will hold the pair together – 'tied' in effect until that bulb deflates when the union concludes. Some people wonder why dog and bitch come tail-to-tail when mating. It is believed that the position taken is some provision of Nature for a mating pair in the wild state. A dog and a bitch so occupied and placed in this way have a biting armament at both ends; not only this, but they can travel their armament in a complete circle. Thus, any attacker at such an inconvenient time can be reasonably well withstood and the pair are far less vulnerable than if their joint backs were turned just one way against any onslaught.

It might be of interest to some that artificial insemination is available in the canine world as indeed it is to humans. In this process, living semen (the fluid containing the spermatozoa) is drawn off from the stud dog then passed by artificial means into the vaginal passage of the bitch at the time of her oestral peak. It is necessary to obtain Kennel Club permission to do this in order that any progeny from a mating by artificial insemination can be exhibited. This rule applies to Kennel Clubs in all countries and a certificate from a competent and qualified veterinary surgeon to the effect that the work has been carried out properly would be required. The system has its advantages in that semen contained in special vials can be flown by air to bitches resident in other lands, allowing them the privilege of acquiring the services of noted stud dogs abroad without the irritation and expense of quarantine restrictions and import licences.

The table on page 74 gives date of mating with expected date of whelping, based on the conventional sixty-three day period.

The bitch in whelp

Many breeders prefer to worm their bitches prior to a mating. This cannot be a bad idea and the breeder should then administer a reliable vermifuge or recommended veterinary medicine which will do the work not later than one week after the end of her season. The normal period of gestation is sixty-three days, although deliveries a few days before or after the anticipated whelping date are by no means uncommon. Such extended periods may be as much as five days either side, sometimes longer. Early puppies may well arrive sound and healthy, but may also evince some indications of their lateness by backward development equivalent to the number of days lost in their dam's womb. However, this need occasion no worry for they will speedily pick up lost ground. In such early examples of this kind it is quite possible that instead of the puppies' eyes opening on the conventional tenth day, they will not open until the thirteenth or fourteenth day of their lives. Early litters sometimes occur with bitches whelping for the first time.

Exercise of the bitch in whelp should be normal up to within a fortnight of the big day when delivery is expected. After this time the

Table showing when a bitch is due to whelp

Served Jan.	Whelps March	Served Feb.	Whelps April	Served March	Whelps May	Served April	Whelps June	Served May	Whelps July	Served June	Whelps Aug.	Served July	Whelps Sept.	Served Aug.	Whelps Oct.	Served Sept.	Whelps Nov.	Served Oct.	Whelps Dec.	Served Nov.	Whelps Jan.	Served Dec.	Whelps Feb.
1	5	1	5	1	3	1	3	1	3	1	3	1	2	1	3	1	3	1	3	1	3	1	2
2	6	2	6	2	4	2	4	2	4	2	4	2	3	2	4	2	4	2	4	2	4	2	3
3	7	3	7	3	5	3	5	3	5	3	5	3	4	3	5	3	5	3	5	3	5	3	4
4	8	4	8	4	6	4	6	4	6	4	6	4	5	4	6	4	6	4	6	4	6	4	5
5	9	5	9	5	7	5	7	5	7	5	7	5	6	5	7	5	7	5	7	5	7	5	6
6	10	6	10	6	8	6	8	6	8	6	8	6	7	6	8	6	8	6	8	6	8	6	7
7	11	7	11	7	9	7	9	7	9	7	9	7	8	7	9	7	9	7	9	7	9	7	8
8	12	8	12	8	10	8	10	8	10	8	10	8	9	8	10	8	10	8	10	8	10	8	9
9	13	9	13	9	11	9	11	9	11	9	11	9	10	9	11	9	11	9	11	9	11	9	10
10	14	10	14	10	12	10	12	10	12	10	12	10	11	10	12	10	12	10	12	10	12	10	11
11	15	11	15	11	13	11	13	11	13	11	13	11	12	11	13	11	13	11	13	11	13	11	12
12	16	12	16	12	14	12	14	12	14	12	14	12	13	12	14	12	14	12	14	12	14	12	13
13	17	13	17	13	15	13	15	13	15	13	15	13	14	13	15	13	15	13	15	13	15	13	14
14	18	14	18	14	16	14	16	14	16	14	16	14	15	14	16	14	16	14	16	14	16	14	15
15	19	15	19	15	17	15	17	15	17	15	17	15	16	15	17	15	17	15	17	15	17	15	16
16	20	16	20	16	18	16	18	16	18	16	18	16	17	16	18	16	18	16	18	16	18	16	17
17	21	17	21	17	19	17	19	17	19	17	19	17	18	17	19	17	19	17	19	17	19	17	18
18	22	18	22	18	20	18	20	18	20	18	20	18	19	18	20	18	20	18	20	18	20	18	19
19	23	19	23	19	21	19	21	19	21	19	21	19	20	19	21	19	21	19	21	19	21	19	20
20	24	20	24	20	22	20	22	20	22	20	22	20	21	20	22	20	22	20	22	20	22	20	21
21	25	21	25	21	23	21	23	21	23	21	23	21	22	21	23	21	23	21	23	21	23	21	22
22	26	22	26	22	24	22	24	22	24	22	24	22	23	22	24	22	24	22	24	22	24	22	23
23	27	23	27	23	25	23	25	23	25	23	25	23	24	23	25	23	25	23	25	23	25	23	24
24	28	24	28	24	26	24	26	24	26	24	26	24	25	24	26	24	26	24	26	24	26	24	25
25	29	25	29	25	27	25	27	25	27	25	27	25	26	25	27	25	27	25	27	25	27	25	26
26	30	26	30	26	28	26	28	26	28	26	28	26	27	26	28	26	28	26	28	26	28	26	27
27	31	27	1	27	29	27	29	27	29	27	29	27	28	27	29	27	29	27	29	27	29	27	28
28	1	28	2	28	30	28	30	28	30	28	30	28	29	28	30	28	30	28	30	28	30	28	1
29	2	29	3	29	31	29	1	29	31	29	31	29	30	29	31	29	1	29	31	29	31	29	2
30	3			30	1	30	2	30	1	30	1	30	1	30	1	30	2	30	2	30	1	30	3
31	4			31	2			31	2			31	2	31	2			31	2			31	4

walks should be easier and perhaps slower. Such exuberances as jumping and rough play should be discouraged and her feeding should be such as to maintain her good condition and allow enough extra nourishment (including calcium phosphate sources) to help with the development of the puppies to come. It has been found useful with a bitch shortly to whelp to give a small teaspoonful of medicinal paraffin every day. This will keep her bowels open and oil her up nicely inside. Such a course need be only a short one and should not commence much more than ten days before the whelping date. Just before the time, the bitch's food should be reduced a little and her feeds staggered. Some novice breeders worry a lot at this time, but there is no reason to envisage any difficulties arising with whelping, especially if the expected birth is from a sound, acknowledged good whelping family of bitches. However, it is always a good thing to be prepared for the occasional situation which might cause some awkward moments and be forewarned by being forearmed with first aid remedies.

Whelping box

Make sure you have a good whelping box ready for the bitch to nest in. If you do not, she is quite capable of making her own selection of a suitable place for her puppies to settle in. This might be in the centre of the bed in your master bedroom, underneath your dining room table or below your prize rose bush at the far end of your garden, in fact, any place likely to prove difficult to oust her from once whelping has started! The whelping box shown in the accompanying diagram will give some idea as to what should be made ready. A sort of 'pig-rail' should be screwed in

WHELPING BOX

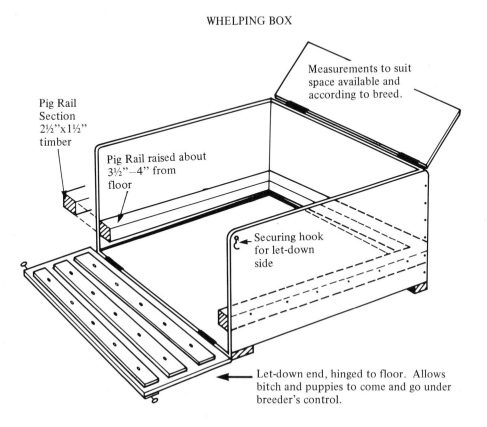

Measurements to suit space available and according to breed.

Pig Rail Section 2½"x1½" timber

Pig Rail raised about 3½"—4" from floor

Securing hook for let-down side

Let-down end, hinged to floor. Allows bitch and puppies to come and go under breeder's control.

round the inner sides this being a valuable adjunct which will prevent puppies from being squashed by a clumsy mother. The rail itself should allow ample room for the whelps to shelter beneath its projection with the bitch herself leaning against it. The lid when closed, makes a raised platform for the dam to jump on to avoid her youngsters' attentions during the latter part of the suckling period and when weaning has commenced. The drop-front of the box, which is ribbed with slats, will permit the breeder to control the comings and goings of the pups when they have reached the walking stage. The suggested measurements have been indicated to make comfortable the average Cairn Terrier bitch and her brood. The sketch is intended as a general idea for a whelping box and the breeder who is a useful hand at woodwork will be able to modify and improve on this to suit his own ideas and convenience. In the matter of bedding, if any is used absolute hygeine must be observed. Personally, I would not use any bedding, but some people like to use sheets of newsprint during the whelping time. This can be laid down loose and exchanged speedily for frequent disposal at this messy time and can be recommended. Others like to use a disinfected piece of new hessian or crash material. This must be nailed securely to the baseboard of the box with strong flat-headed nails which cannot be dislodged when the bitch begins to scratch. Avoid at all costs deep layers of hay or straw under which whelps could snuggle and be smothered. The same danger exists with the use of blankets and soft linings.

The bitch should be introduced to these new quarters a good week before the event, so that by the time she whelps she will have become used to her new surroundings away from the family circle and ready to commence her maternal duties without any distractions.

4 Whelping and After-care

The bitch's temperature when about to whelp will usually drop below 37.7°C (100°F) even to 36.4°C (97.5°F). This should be a fair indication to the breeder that labour pains are imminent. The bitch will probably refuse food and drink at this stage and show some agitation in preparing her nest, scratching and swivelling round on herself in typical pre-whelping fashion. Just before she whelps she may relax into a profound sleep, this being Nature's way of preparing her for the onerous period ahead. The wise breeder will ensure at this stage that noisy children and curious well-wishers are kept at a distance so as not to disturb her.

Preparations will have been made for the whelping and the breeder should have warned his veterinary surgeon in advance and asked him to be ready to come out should complications ensue. Secondly, he should have provided himself with a good emergency first-aid kit. Some breeders will have had prior experience in such matters and will know what items may be required, but for the newcomer to the exercise, a good guide would be:

1   Packet of fairly large disposable tissues.
2   Sharp sterilised scissors, probe-end surgical type is preferable.
3   Surgical thread or strong cotton to pre-cut length, about 7 in (18 cm).
4   Vaseline and a liquid antiseptic, as free from strong aroma as possible.
5   Clean towel for drying hands, and pieces of clean towelling.
6   Well-scoured clean basin and a covered stone hot-water bottle.
7   Emergency feeding bottle.
8   Quantity of brandy, which if required, should be doled out *very* sparingly, i.e. a drop or two at a time in a teaspoon.
9   A Thermos flask containing warm milk and a saucer bowl.
10 Personal necessities required by breeder, drink, food, reading material, etc.

When the bitch is about to whelp she will evince a slight straining or rippling along her back. These are the muscles flexing and it may not be repeated immediately, but will come on more frequently and the

Ch. Saucy Miss of Monary, owned by Mrs M. Shuttleworth. (*J. Sedley*)

straining become more apparent until there are three or four strains at intervals of about the same number of minutes. Probably at this time the first warm milk drink should be given to the bitch to hasten progress, but she may refuse it, in which case do not press her, leaving her alone. If however, the animal is already very late in producing her puppies and the breeder is experiencing some real anxiety as to her welfare, then it will be wise to call in the veterinary surgeon without delay. Puppies are born one by one and are presented head first, this being the normal mode of delivery. However, those that come rear end first need occasion no alarm, unless the dam seems distressed, in which case she may need some assistance. Rear-end first birth is known as 'breech' birth and can prove awkward, but not necessarily. If manual assistance is given to a bitch struggling with a breech birth every time she strains, the problem is usually soon disposed of; it is mostly the brachycephalic breeds, such as the Pugs, Pekingese and Bulldogs – those with large heads and flat faces and small pubic apertures which experience more serious trouble. Every bitch has to be assessed on her merits or demerits. This is when a breeder's experience will tell him what action to take. Any form of interference during whelping is undesirable and it is best always to let Nature take its course. Only when commonsense tells you that the situation looks critical should veterinary help be employed.

Maiden bitches sometimes need special attention. Occasionally, a maiden bitch will panic at the sight of her first puppy, or be distraught with her labour pains, symptoms not hitherto experienced. Sometimes a bitch will make no effort to produce her puppies and lie dormant when the first puppy appears at her rear end. Should this happen, the breeder must take one of the pieces of clean towelling he has had standing by and grip and newborn puppy gently, easing it out of its dam in rhythm with her straining. The puppies should then follow in sequence each in its own liquid-filled sac (*placenta*). The experienced bitch will break the water-sac herself and this must be done to allow the youngster to inhale air into its lungs. Failure to do this will cause the puppy to expire. The bitch should then buffet her puppy with her tongue, applying what is really a form of artificial respiration. If she does not do this, the breeder must apply some firm massaging to the puppy's body and it may be necessary to give it a bit of a shaking to ensure its throat is clear of mucus. The bitch will then start to clean up the puppy with some vigorous licking which will remove any of this unwanted slime around its mouth. The dam should also nip the umbilical cord which connects the whelp to the placenta or afterbirth which at this stage should be still inside her. If she does not appear to be dispelling the placenta, the cord should be taken carefully between finger and thumb and *gently* pulled to withdraw the afterbirth from the bitch. Do not pull from the direction of the puppy itself. Any tug which puts a drag away from the puppy's navel will probably cause an umbilical hernia. This, quite apart from being a disfigurement in later life might well necessitate a minor operation to disperse it. Tie a piece of your surgical thread or strong cotton about $\frac{1}{2}$ in ($1\frac{1}{4}$ cm) away from the puppy's navel. Cut the umbilical cord at a short point, $1\frac{1}{2}$ in (3.15 cm) above and beyond the tie with your sterilised scissors or nip it with well-scrubbed finger and thumb nails.

The placenta should then be disposed of, although some bitches eat this, it being an instinctive action which animals inherit from the wild state to give them sustenance. Temporarily incapacitated at such a time she would be unlikely to obtain food for twenty-four hours until able and free to leave her whelps and get food for herself. However, assuming she has not disposed of the placentae, it is rather important for the domestic breeder to keep a count on the number of these as they are expelled. Once whelping is over they should be checked and their total made to correspond with the number of puppies born. Should it be apparent that a placenta has been retained by the bitch in her womb, then it will be advisable to call the veterinary surgeon who will expel it effectively with a suitable injection. By so doing it will probably save the bitch from a septic womb infection, not uncommon in cases of after-birth retention.

Providing the pattern of whelping follows this straightforward form there is little to worry about. Between deliveries of her puppies the bitch will probably have short sleeps, then wake up, start straining again, and so on. Should she suddenly appear to slacken her efforts and the straining becomes noticeably weaker while it is obvious that some puppies remain in her, this could suggest uterine inertia necessitiating a Caesarean section operation (see p. 87). However, Cairn Terriers are not particularly prone to such problems and providing the bitch is well made, healthy, and comes from a good whelping strain, no such worrying situation should arise.

A normal whelping would take about three to four hours during which time she should be encouraged to take a few warm milk drinks. If possible, get her outside to relieve herself, although she may not do this willingly. Many breeders remove the puppies one after the other, as they are born, and place them in an open top carton with a well-wrapped-round stone hot water bottle. Later, when the puppies have been put on to their dam, once you have had a chance to clean up the whelping box, they will begin to suckle. At this stage, the bitch should be left alone and neither animals nor children allowed near to disturb her. A darkened room is best for her and no one, except the breeder perhaps, should handle the whelps except in the initial stages for sexing them. She will

A pannier of fine Cairn Terrier puppies bred by Patrick Rimer.

need a lot of sleep now after such exhaustive efforts and some breeders instruct their veterinary surgeon to inject the dam at this time with penicillin. This contributes to inner cleanliness and gives some peace of mind in that no infection will develop as a result of the whelping and consequent lowering of the bitch's resistance.

The ideal litter will number five to six. Five is possibly better for these will thrive remarkably well on the average milk supply from a Cairn nursing mother, whereas bigger litters not only absorb more but are slower to develop. They are also more likely to lower the dam's constitution. Close attention must be given to any members of the litter who seem weaker than the others to ensure they are not ousted from the main inguinal teats which lie towards the groin area; these being the most prolific with milk. If the litter has proved an extra large one and it is felt the bitch cannot cope properly with it, or looks like being an indifferent mother, then a foster parent may have to be considered. Some bitches do not produce their milk very quickly and with the puppies screaming for food and nothing forthcoming, both dam and owner are liable to become distressed. A veterinary surgeon will be able to deal with the hastening of milk flow, but if there seems a wide divergence between the number of puppies and the amount of milk to feed them, this will be a further reason for introducing a foster mother to the scene. The canine weekly journals usually indicate where these can be obtained and certain kennels specialise in their supply being noted for clean and reliable bitches. The Collie breeds are usually well endowed with milk and make good fosters, but whether pure-bred or mongrels, their breeding is unimportant so long as ample milk is flowing to rear your puppies and the dam-to-be is healthy.

Foster mothers

The usual procedure of kennels which specialise in these foster parents is to use a bitch, frequently of doubtful origin, allow her to produce puppies, then dispose of them as soon as there is a call on her services from a person or kennel with a pedigree litter which has been rejected by its mother, or for some other breeding problem. Quite apart from the distress which is occasioned upon the foster parent bitch by having her own puppies removed from her and she herself being consigned on possibly a long trip in an uncomfortable container to a strange and distant home, there exists also the danger that she might bring in some infection to the pedigree litter. The business of acquiring and using a foster mother is expensive in itself; if she should bring in some disease that kills off your pedigree litter than she is worse than expensive, although it is no fault of her own, poor creature. Any breeder envisaging the use of a foster parent should ensure that its health and antecedents have been checked and approved by a qualified veterinary surgeon before she leaves her own locality.

The introduction of the whelps to a foster dam must be handled with utmost circumspection. She might be reluctant to accept her new charges, especially if she has several of her own snuggling to her body. Carefully remove two of her pups, also the blanket on which she is resting. Take the whelps out of sight and sound of their dam and rub them up against two of the pedigree puppies so that the scent of the former settles on to the latter. They must then be put with the other puppies and left together for about half-an-hour. Then, by removing the foster-mother from her bed at intervals, the pedigree youngsters which require her attention can be 'smuggled' into her bed by the time she returns.

Close watch must be kept on her to ensure that she accepts the newcomers without annoyance. A method to encourage her in this scheme is to smear something sweet on their coats which she will lick off and thereby welcome their intrusion. Once the new puppies start suckling most of the problems will have been disposed of, but it remains necessary to keep a watchful eye on proceedings until it is certain that all is well in the nest. Any sign of distress or discomfort from the dam must be dealt with immediately, as her peace of mind is essential if the puppies are to thrive.

It is worth bearing in mind the possible need of a foster-mother if your Cairn bitch has a bad record as a mother. If this is the case, it will be as well to make prior arrangements for a foster to be standing by at the expected date of the whelping.

Dew claws

All puppies are born with these rudimentary digits which are somewhat similar to the thumb in humans. They appear invariably on the forelegs, sometimes on the hind legs. The latter are always removed because they are objectionable; those on the fore limbs because it is breed practice and in any case, they often constitute a hazard to the dog in the field. It is easy enough for him to get them caught up when rummaging in thick terrain and tear his flesh. Remove them when the puppy is about 3 days old, certainly not much later, providing the puppy is thriving. Make sure the dam is out of earshot when the job is done for any whimpers may distress her.

The task is a simple one; it can be done by a veterinary surgeon if you doubt your own competence, but if you tackle the job yourself, then a pair of straight snub-nosed scissors must be sterilised and a few pads of lint or cotton wool got ready. Cut down with the scissors close to the limb. An assistant to stretch out the puppy's leg can be a help if you feel a little nervous but one soon becomes adept. Once the appendage has been removed press on one of the swabs which has been dipped in Friar's Balsam or similar antiseptic such as crystals of permanganate of potash. These are obtainable from any chemist and are useful kennel stock items. It is unlikely that the puppy will be caused much pain; a whelp might whimper a little but most appear indifferent. When you have completed the task check all the wounds to ensure bleeding is under control and make periodical checks twice daily until they have healed nicely.

Never leave dew claws on a dog up to adult stage as to remove them from a mature specimen will necessitate an anaesthetic probably requiring professional assistance.

Feeding the dam

For at least a day your Cairn mother should have nothing but nourishing milk drinks. There are some excellent sustained milk foods on the market and these are ideal for the purpose. Frequency of feeding is usually about five times a day, but of course, the manufacturer's suggestions must be followed. A little raw meat can follow providing her temperature is normal, but once it fluctuates then back to milk foods she should go. A recommended diet for the nursing bitch would be:

    7 am   Sustained milk drink of a proprietary make
   10 am   Meat (raw) chopped small
    1 pm   Scrambled or poached egg with wheatmeal bread

4 pm   Milk food as at 7 am
7 pm   Raw meat again or carefully boned boiled fish
10 pm   Milk food as at 7 am and 4 pm.

The quantity and distribution of the bitch's meals will depend largely on the size of her litter. The purpose of the feeding is not only to satisfy her, but to charge her with health and goodness which she can pass down to her puppies in the form of milk. A bitch with a full complement of puppies will obviously need proportionately more food than one with just two or three youngsters to feed. If she is nursing a biggish litter of say seven then it might be advisable to give her an extra drink in the early hours for a few days following the whelping. Her own milk supply will be best built up with cold water and raw meat – these are the best producers for milk quantity and quality – but if diarrhoea is noted, and this is common enough in a bitch after whelping, cut down the volume of milk and give more water. It is also advisable that her meat intake should be reduced for the time being until the condition has eased off.

Post-whelping problems

ECLAMPSIA
It is not uncommon for a bitch to be found to be very excitable after she has whelped. She will whine and give every indication of nervous distress with some panting. She may transport her puppies from here to there without apparent reason. The breeder's first action should be to confine her to a darkened room and give her as much reassurance and sympathetic attention as possible. The condition is known as Eclampsia and is common enough as a condition in nursing bitches, being caused by a sudden deficiency of calcium in the blood. This has been caused by the heavy demand placed upon her reserves of milk, now considerably depleted. It is usually the mature bitch which suffers from this condition rather than one with her first litter, although any bitch with a large litter can be affected. The initial symptoms are a change in expression, the bitch giving the impression of being dazed and uncertain of herself with some staggering and twitching of the front limbs. Panting and general distress are further symptoms and your veterinary surgeon will probably inject the patient with a preparation strong in calcium and phosphorus combined with Vitamin-D to counteract her calcium deficiencies and curb the excitability. Relief is usually apparent within a few minutes and after half-an-hour the bitch should be back to normal.

If possible, give her a rest away from her puppies, but she may refuse to cooperate with you in this move. In many cases it is advisable to give the puppies supplementary feeds of proprietary milk, mixed according to the maker's directions for their size and age. The bitch may require, at your veterinary surgeon's discretion, a further injection, but in any case, she should be kept under constant supervision for Eclampsia is a very disturbing condition in a bitch. It may result in some of the puppies being trampled, so disorientated might the bitch become in her conduct. The supplementary feeding given to the puppies will help to ease the reduction of the calcium from her mother. Some breeders theorise that Eclampsia could be prevented in many cases if the bitch is removed progressively from her puppies for longer and longer periods each day. This would possibly be three or four minutes in the third day and increasing every day until at a month the bitch would be away for periods of several hours at a time over the day. These periods away from the puppies should be accompanied by exercise in the fresh air, running after a ball, etc. Most breeders will almost certainly follow this procedure to a greater or lesser degree, in any case. But equally, the bitch should never be forced to stay away from her puppies if this seems to upset her. The very fact of her becoming upset and anxious could well bring on an attack of Eclampsia, so her feelings have to be considered important at such a time. If an attack of Eclampsia seems imminent – for instance, if the bitch begins to pant suddenly and without apparent reason, whimpers, scratches in corners or tries to carry a puppy around in her mouth – then she will need further treatment until she is calm. There are suitable preparations on the market which deal adequately and well with this condition and one such should be kept ready to use if needed; but the size of the dose should be prescribed by your veterinary surgeon. Such elixirs as 'Cal-D' and 'Stress' are noted for their usefulness in the treatment of Eclampsia. All patients when treated should be kept in a warm environment.

EXCESS MILK

Sometimes a whelping mother has too much milk, the surplus not having been taken up quickly enough by her puppies. The congestion which ensues exudes and cakes over the breasts. Those teats affected are usually the inguinals, i.e. the large ones at the rear in the groin area. These become over-gorged with milk, inflamed and cause the dam a great deal of discomfort. In her irritation she will gnaw at them and in an advanced state abscesses will form. To offset this, if you have a bitch showing signs of excess milk, relieve her condition by gently kneading and milking the nipples; and this will cut down her fluid supply substantially. The only danger involved in dispersing a bitch's milk in this way is that it encourages more to come. However, this situation is usually rectified by the puppies themselves as they grow on, for they are able to take more from her and by so doing create a better balance. In the case of a bitch who has lost her puppies and is carrying milk to her bodily discomfort, then veterinary advice is best sought as there are suitable drugs to offset this state. Sometimes breeders are worried at seeing their bitches with milk after the puppies have been weaned. It is seldom that this condition need cause concern as the surplus will usually disperse naturally as the glands tighten up. Some breeders hasten this process by dabbing around the teat area with methylated spirits soaked into a wad of cotton wool and this seems an effective system.

AGLACTICA

The lack of milk is a somewhat different story and a worrying one for the breeder with a very promising litter, also for the dam herself. It is not uncommon for the whelping mother to get a high temperature and this often stays the flow of her milk for as much as thirty-six hours. Puppies need their mother's milk almost as soon as they are born if they are to thrive well. If the milkless state persists longer than six hours then urgent action has to be taken, apart from the constant placing of the puppies on the teats to encourage milk flow. It is important that the whelps get the *colostrum* which is present in their dam's milk in the early stages of its flow. This is Nature's immuniser and gives the puppies protection from disease in the first few weeks of their lives. If they fail to get this colostrum then it is better to let your veterinary surgeon take over. He will make the desired injections to give necessary protection at this time. The dam herself may be injected also to reduce her temperature and this treatment usually coincides with an even and normal flow of milk.

Hand-rearing

This is a task for the dedicated breeder only. Sometimes, as already mentioned, a bitch will have no milk to offer, following delivery of her puppies. She may be too ill to know or care what becomes of the youngsters or refuse to attend them for a variety of reasons, probably best known to herself. At worst, she may have died in the course of whelping them or due to an unfortunate Caesarian section. The breeder is then left with an orphan litter, crying out loudly for milk, which cannot be made forthcoming. If he has foreseen such a situation, he will have arranged for a foster-parent to be on the way, but to come by a foster at a moment's notice is no easy task, so the alternative course of action is to hand-feed them. This is by no means as simple as it sounds and the person taking on this work must be prepared for at least a month

Ch. Monary Susanella, owned
by Mrs M. Shuttleworth.
(*Hartley*)

of devoted attention to the puppies and quite a few sleepless nights. However, when the course of care and feeding has been completed and the litter satisfactorily reared, it will be an unusual breeder who does not survey the results of his work with justifiable pride.

A good proprietary puppy milk food prepared to the manufacturer's instructions is a first-class stand-by for bitch's milk. Great care must be taken to prepare this in the exact quantities recommended, also the determination of feeding times and the temperature of the feeds. A fresh mixture is essential for every meal and care must be taken to keep the food at one level of heat while every individual is fed, and this is no easy job when a large litter is involved. The bowl of milk should be kept standing in a pannier of hot water and tested periodically with a thermometer. This will ensure that when the time comes round to feed the last puppy, his or her food will be given at the same required heat as enjoyed by the first feeder.

Once the puppy has been fed, wipe his nose gently with a piece of damp cotton wool. This will remove any congealed milk around his nostrils and face. Normally, if the dam herself was on the scene she would start licking her offspring as soon as they had fed in order to induce urination and the passing of motions. Her wet, warm and bossy tongue around their private parts would soon bring this about naturally, but as these orphans are deprived of such maternal attentions, the result has to be achieved artificially. To simulate the bitch's method it is necessary to take a pad of cotton wool which has been dampened in warm water. Gently stroke over and around the puppies' parts with it and both urination and the passing of motions will be effected. Once this has been proved successful softly smear with 'Vaseline' the anus, also penis or vulva of every puppy. It is important to see that the puppies' intestines do not become blocked, so ensure that *both* motions are passed either before or immediately following a meal. Should any puppy appear distressed by constipation, it may prove necessary to ease into the rectum (for a fractional distance) a well-greased clinical thermometer of the half-minute blunt-end variety. This can be expected to encourage the passing of a motion.

If possible, always use an infra-red lamp when hand-rearing puppies. This maintains a constant temperature and should be set between 24° and 26.5°C (75°–80°F) for the first few days, after which time the warmth emitted from the lamp can be reduced to 15.5°C (60°F) by raising it from floor level and thereby easing off the warmth by going higher each day. Make certain that the lamp is suspended safely from the ceiling and use a dull-emitter bulb as this type is considered safer when youngsters open their eyes, about ten days after birth. It is as well to protect the lamp reflector with an all-round wire cage guard in case a bulb should break loose accidentally and fall on the litter. It will be realised that puppies who have been deprived of their dam's natural milk will lack in the assimilation of colostrum, the protective natural fluid, already referred to. This contains globulin and has the effect of a mild laxative, eliminating impurities which may have accumulated in the puppies during the period of gestation. The antibodies concerned serve to immunise the youngsters against the various virus diseases which beset young canines until they are about nine or ten weeks of age. Hand-reared puppies must therefore be given an alternative form of protection in the form of gamma globulin, and here the veterinary surgeon's skill has to be employed. He will give suitable injections. The task of hand-rearing is a far from easy one and for the truly dedicated breeder who loves his dogs. It takes up considerable time, patience and occasionally it engenders a deal of frustration; but so long as regularity in feeding, correct temperature of food and surroundings, regular defecation and urination are ensured, success can be expected.

Caesarean section

This operation sometimes becomes necessary if the bitch is carrying one or more large puppies or if the puppies are wrongly placed or dead within the womb. The veterinary surgeon will open the uterus and remove the puppies. The danger lies not in the actual operation, which is fairly simple from a veterinary viewpoint, but in the fact that the bitch may be, of necessity, heavily anaesthetised, which means that the unborn puppies are themselves anaesthetised. Being so small and weak at the unborn stage it is often extremely difficult to get them to show signs of life after a birth of this kind by Caesarean section. Many puppies have in the past been lost for just this reason. However, surgeons today use an advanced form of anaesthetic which avoids anaesthetising the youngsters, and this may well be the answer to the loss of so many puppies through this type of operation. The secret of making a successful operation of this kind lies largely in careful timing. The operation is best undertaken (after careful consideration as to its necessity) when the bitch has commenced her labour, but before she becomes panicky by ineffectual and unproductive straining.

   If it is to save a bitch from a very long and arduous whelping, then this operation is to be recommended, for the dam seldom suffers any after-effects apart from a natural 'muzziness' on waking. She is usually soon comfortably settled with her little family, all suckling away happily at her in a matter of two or three hours after the operation. Make sure that all of them are warm and in a quiet place, as there is, of course, a certain amount of shock involved. Some breeders utilise their infra-red lamp, installed in situ for a few days, but it is more usual and possibly preferable to introduce stone hot-water bottles well wrapped round with pieces of blanket to prevent the bitch and her puppies from getting burnt. These should be placed behind her back in the whelping box and a good cosy heat will be generated.

It is not unusual to find this type of operation will prevent or slow up the bitch's milk from coming down for several hours. Should this occur, it may be deemed wise to allow the whelps some interim nourishment from a good milk food preparation. The milk should be made to the consistency specified for new-born puppies, details for mixing being written on the canister. However, in spite of the fact that there is little or no milk coming from their mother's teats, the youngsters should be deployed constantly on the teats as their suckling will certainly stimulate the flow and hurry it along. The fact that the bitch has had the misfortune to suffer a Caesarean section does not mean that she is destined for this inconvenience every time she is due to whelp. Probably next time she is due everything will go off normally with no complications at all.

Infertility

Some breeders worry that their bitches might prove barren or become infertile thereby obstructing their owner's plans and ambitions as a breeder. Such fears can be disproved of course, by trial and error, but infertility is probably due to some defect in either sire or dam, i.e. in the breeding itself and if so, then there is little to be done. More likely, an advanced age in either parent is likely to reduce fertility. Naturally, as an animal ages its reproductive powers abate and frankly, it is not wise to use aged parents in a breeding programme. Neither should a stud dog be used excessively when he is young; he can be brought into the field for regular work when he reaches two years of age. No Cairn Terrier bitch should be mated at her first heat and she should not be given maternal duties on a regular basis until she is well over two years old. Likewise, old parents often produce puppies which lack constitution so where possible always use parental stock which is in the prime of life to produce strong, vigorous youngsters.

Fading puppies

This is another unfortunate condition which can affect an entire litter, or sometimes, just one or two of its members. Although it is fairly common in dogs, little is known of its cause. Some veterinary experts have blamed a dam's poor health and constitution, others claim that the cause lies with faulty environment or bad housing conditions and management at whelping time. The usual symptoms are, that whereas a litter is born apparently lusty and well, some or all of them gradually get weak and unhappy, finally dying off with no apparent cause. The deterioration process may take anything from a few hours after birth to several days.

When fading is suspected, veterinary advice should be sought at once. Certain injections have proved helpful and penicillin has been used with success when infection is suspected, both the dam and her brood being treated at the same time. It has been stated that sometimes the aftermath of Canine Virus Hepatitus being passed down from an affected brood bitch to her offspring is a likely contributor to fading in a litter. This may be just one of the reasons for the tragic loss of youngsters and it emphasises the really urgent need for ensuring that before mating, both parents have been examined and found in first-rate health and free from worms. That the whelping procedure is disciplined and well managed becomes important too – every effort being made to ensure that the bitch's innate whelping functions at this time are not subjected to unnecessary interference by human agency. Her food must be fresh and wholesome; her exercise planned to improve her mental awareness as well as her body.

Worms and worming

It is generally expected that a puppy will have worms, the **roundworm** being the most common in Britain. This is a parasite rather similar in appearance to vermicelli, creamy-yellow in colour and if not expelled quickly it will debilitate the puppy and cause him considerable discomfort. The symptoms are usually diarrhoea of a somewhat jellified consistency, an upset stomach and loss of appetite. However, conversely, in certain cases the puppy becomes quite voracious in his appetite. The incidence of these worms is often revealed by the way a puppy will rotate on his rear end or squat down suddenly as though irritated in that region. There are a number of good proprietary vermifuges and vermicides on the market and these are excellent and one should be used when the puppy is about five weeks of age, or according to the maker's instructions. The worms are usually expelled in a tight coil and once these have been eliminated the puppy will build up and thrive speedily. Many breeders dose their bitches ten days after mating as they believe the eggs of the roundworm pass from the dam through the placenta to infect the puppies even while they are in the womb.

Other worms to watch for are **tape worms** which are usually noted in short segments adhering to the puppy's anal region. These segments look like grains of rice, but when the worm itself is expended it can be several feet long and like a length of creamy tape, from which it gets its name. **Hook worms** are seldom found in the U.K. being common enough in the United States, however. Your veterinary surgeon will be able to deal with the last two offenders with appropriate drugs. It must be remembered that any puppy having been wormed should be kept warm and free from draughts.

Breeding terms

This is an arrangement made between two people, the breeder, instead of selling his bitch puppy outright transferring it to another person. He does this because he may not wish to relinquish his controlling ownership of a bitch whose strain is valuable to him in his breeding plans. By passing over to another person, a puppy he cannot accommodate or afford to run on himself he arranges with the custodian to keep her and breed from her under his direction. In doing this, he either hands over the bitch for no charge or for a nominal sum, instead of the fee she would have sold for as a promising puppy. The arrangement usually made is that when she is bred from and produces a litter then a number of puppies from this litter, and possibly subsequent litters will have to be handed over to the original breeder.

Such an arrangement as this needs to be conducted with great care. In fact, the Kennel Club have a system whereby the plan can be officially recorded on their registry, *viz* 'Registration of the Loan or Use of a Bitch for Breeding Purposes'. The arrangement is thus recorded and a date is determined for its termination. It is important that the bitch goes to a good and kind home where her interests will be looked after and the arrangements made will be adhered to properly and honestly. It is usual for the bitch's custodian to keep the bitch after the term of the plan has been satisfactorily concluded.

Both people involved in an arrangement like this should realise it is fraught with some risk and the conditions drawn up between them should be mutually acceptable from the outset. It is often an excellent opportunity for a person who lacks finance to acquire a good bitch to breed from, and learn from, in the course of breeding good stock without capital outlay.

5 Feeding and Management

Weaning

The way a Cairn is weaned will have a lasting effect on him all his life. It is of vital importance to a breeder to ensure that this work is carried out with care and a deal of dedication. With such attention a strong, healthy dog will be put on to the right path and one so started seldom suffers a set-back, even in the difficult days of adolescence. You should start the weaning process when the puppy is between three and four weeks of age. This applies to a puppy from an average-sized litter of five or six members. If the litter is by chance larger than this then it might be wise to start soon after three weeks of age. Much will depend on the flow of milk coming through from the dam. If this is adequate then your start can be more gradual in its nature.

The puppy must be taught to lap. There are a number of good proprietary brands of baby milk on the market and your chemist or veterinary surgeon will recommend one. Instructions for using it will be found on the packet or tin, and this can be adapted to suit any age and weight of puppy. Normally, a heaped teaspoonful will do as a starter for each puppy and it should be mixed with hot water just off boiling point to the consistency of thick cream then beaten or stirred until it appears glossy and emulsified. Then bring it to the consistency of thin cream by adding more hot water. Four or five teaspoons of the mixture brought to blood heat should then be put into a saucer and placed on a clean towel. Then, push the puppy's nose gently into the mixture. At first, he will not like it and splutter and blow into it; then as the taste of the food begins to register with him he will show more interest, especially if a little is taken up on your finger and placed between his lips. Once he has overcome this initial difficulty of lapping he will soon attack his food with relish. Try and maintain the temperature of his food at blood heat by standing its container in a pan of hot water during the meal time. Once the lapping is under way, firmer food like light milk puddings, poached egg, minced boiled tripe and finely shredded raw butcher's meat can be introduced.

So that the puppy starts off his weaning with a good appetite make sure that he has been off and away from his dam for at least two hours

Ch. Camcairn Cordelia,
owned by Messrs.
Cammish & Williams.
(*Garwood*)

previously. Then he will attack his food with gusto and begin to look forward to this 'new' menu. Goat's milk can be used later instead of cow's milk and the value of this cannot be over-emphasised in view of its high fat and mineral salts content. Cow's milk is good, but it is of secondary value and should never be diluted. An appreciation of the great differences between bitches' milk and that of goats and cows is shown by the analyses published in Clifford Hubbard's *The Complete Dog Breeders' Manual* 1954, and used in several of my books on various breeds. Here is the table:

ANALYSES OF MILK

Animal	Sugar	Casein etc	Fat	Salts	Water
DOG	3.1	8.0	12.0	1.2	75.5
GOAT	4.75	4.0	6.25	1.0	84.0
CAT	5.2	7.9	3.65	0.9	82.35
COW	4.85	3.75	3.7	0.6	87.1
SHEEP	4.95	4.7	5.2	0.7	84.45

No doubt up to the end of the first week of solid feeding the puppies will have been fed individually, but it will be found that by careful guidance, early communal feeding can be achieved. To avoid some of the more eager ones from falling head-first into the food, it is a good idea to raise the bowl perhaps a couple of inches off ground level. It will be found that some individuals will seek to hog the main part of the food and when this is noted you can allow the greedy one or two to get their reasonable share then withdraw them from the scene, leaving the way clear for their slower brothers and sisters to eat.

After ten days of weaning as a team, the puppies should be approaching complete independence from their dam; in fact, the greater their solid food intake the less they will, in fact, depend on her and when they are five weeks of age her influence upon them will be negligible. She may make a visit to them once a day when they will probably rush her and grab an impromptu meal from her now-failing milk supply. The dam will soon want to see them off however, for their bulk and strength, not to speak of their sharp claws will be irritating her. By this time too, they will be on five proper meals a day, two or three milky ones and two with raw meat. The quantities should be staggered well to avoid distension of their stomach muscles and a close watch should be kept on the bitch when she is near to her puppies in case she regurgitates or disgorges her own food to help in the weaning process. To some, this might appear an unsavoury system of mothercare, but it is a perfectly natural function on the bitch's part and unlikely to do any harm to the youngsters unless one encounters a morsel too large for its gullet. The main thing to do is to ensure that the bitch gets another meal to replace what she has brought up, for after doing this service she is bound to become hungry.

Now is the time to commence fattening the mother up. A lot of her strength and body will have gone into her puppies and her resilience will have been lessened quite considerably. She should be given plenty of fresh, raw meat, eggs, cheese and biscuits, but her fluid intake should be reduced to a minimum to help the natural diminishment of her milk supply until it finally disappears. A tonic will help her too and there are proprietary medicines on the market which are good, or your veterinary surgeon will prescribe one. Many breeders forget to work on the dam at this time, so preoccupied are they with their valuable new arrivals. To omit this husbandry shows lack of planning skill, especially if it is contemplated mating the bitch again at next heat.

Novice breeders are often puzzled as to the amount of meat to give a young puppy. As a rough, but useful guide, the amount at each meal should not exceed the bulk of each puppy's head. Imagine the food roughly shaped or moulded into a ball about the size of the youngster's head and skull. When the food is put down watch him tackle it. If he goes through the quantity comfortably, then no doubt it suits his appetite, but if he pauses, takes a breath, then starts again, it is reasonably certain that this puppy needs only this quantity or just a little more food up to the point where he paused. If you experiment in this way, you will soon have skill in assessing your puppies' requirements as they go along. At six weeks of age, the growing puppy can have Farley's Rusks, biscuits etc, as well as his normal diet.

Camcairn Claudius, owned by
Mrs D. Waine. (*J. Dixon*)

Never overlook additives which are of use to a youngster's well-being, but use them with circumspection and in moderation. For example, with a youngster making bone, as he is at this time, you can sprinkle a little powdered calcium over his main meal. This can be obtained from a reliable pharmacist or your veterinary surgeon, either of whom will suggest the amount to use. Concentrate on those foods which are strong in calcium and phosphorus. Introduce Vitamin-D, the 'sunshine' Vitamin, found in fish oils (especially halibut-liver oil), egg yolk, butter and liver. Vitamin-A is useful too and this is obtainable from liquid obtained by boiling endives, carrots, watercress and turnip tops, this is poured over one of the meat meals. A more comprehensive survey of Vitamins, their content and usage will be found at the end of this section. The clever breeder will incorporate a proper balance of Vitamins and minerals in his application to preserve good all-round health in his Cairn. So long as the dog is allowed fresh meat, fish, milk and eggs with easy access to sunshine and clean, green grass grazing, he is unlikely to go wrong in health. Some meat fat will benefit him as this is strong in Vitamins A and D. There are good proprietary conditioners on the market in the form of yeast tablets. These contain Vitamins and minerals blended for puppy, dog and brood bitch alike.

Once your puppy has been fed on food other than his dam's milk she will stop cleaning him up. This job must be undertaken by the breeder who should ensure that any motions left adhering to the anal region are cleaned off with cotton wool swabs to which have been added a few drops of 'TCP' or similar preparation.

Most Cairn puppies are big enough and fit enough to go off to their new homes by the time they are eight weeks of age; some breeders prefer to leave them at the kennel for another fortnight. You can, in deference to the dam's feelings, stagger their departures, but this only assumes that she is still showing some interest in them, and does not want to lose them all at once. The wise owner, knowing his bitch will have to make his own decision as to what is best for her. Most, if not all, bitches are usually quite pleased to see the backs of their brood by the time eight weeks has passed!

Puppy diet sheets

Always make sure that the new owners of your puppies have suitable diet sheets. Even owners who have prior experience of puppy rearing should have one, for it is easy to forget the art and routine. Lists of recommended foods and feeding times are always appreciated and it is important to know how and on what a new puppy has been fed, so that the sudden change of ownership is not made too dramatic. A simple feeding programme for a Cairn Terrier puppy is given below:

Breakfast 8.30 am Bread and milk, cereal and milk, light porridge etc. The milk should be just warm, never hot. Alternate with a scrambled egg or steamed white fish. Rusks baked in the oven are very good. These can be put in the milk and sweetened with honey or glucose.

Lunchtime 12.30 pm Chopped meat meal, beef, chicken, rabbit (bone carefully, these last two) good offal, mixed with wholemeal, oatmeal, brown bread rusks soaked in 'Oxo' or 'Bovril' gravy. A little grated carrot or Cheddar cheese can top the meal. Cottage cheese is good in small amounts.

Teatime 4.30 pm Similar to the breakfast meal or warm milk with rusks and gravy. Additives such as Benger's Food or Slippery Elm are recommended in light portions.

Dinnertime 8.30 pm Repeat as for the lunchtime meal, chopped meat meal with broth or gravy.

Meat should be chopped small to a useful size, but not minced. Some breeders shred it, but better results are achieved when the dog's gastric juices are given full play. Minced meat may not fully accomplish this, but care is needed to ensure the pieces chopped are not too chunky as some youngsters, being greedy, could choke on large pieces.

Progressive feeding has now to be considered. The puppy is now making bone and muscle. At four months, say, he can take more food in proportion and as you taper down the small puppy feeding schedule, he should be on three adequate meals a day, taking care that he does not appear too distended after his meals. He is adding weight quickly at this stage and he is approaching the age of complete dentition. This is a critical time for him and the next three months are often painful. Also, his resistance may be lowered and lay him open to any disease which may be about. This means that his food should be of the best quality to ensure he is kept in prime condition.

He is by now making his preferences in the choice of food and before he begins to show too many 'fads' in the way of his meals, it is a good idea to get him used to a variety of foods, i.e. raw meat, cooked meat (not too much of this), boiled, also steamed fish, proprietary canned meats, (good and recommended processed forms), various biscuits and so on. Horsemeat should be avoided really, unless you encounter an emergency which demands improvisation and then it should be boiled as should any animal feeding meats. By giving your dog such a variety you ensure against him becoming fastidious and turning up his nose at anything but raw meat. When a dog rejects any food but his favourite meals, it becomes a worry to feed him for it is not always practicable or convenient to produce just what he wants for every meal. This is why a dog should be trained in feeding just as he is for other things. Be careful with rabbit; the flesh is highly nutritive, but it should be eaten immediately after the animal has been killed, for the bones are springy and dangerous following the first day. Never allow the dog to have poultry or game to eat unless you have boned it with great care. The bones are needle-like and many a dog has choked on these, or had his gullet pierced. During winter months always pour a teaspoonful of coarse cod-liver oil on the dog's food and in the summer do the same thing with a little olive oil which is less heating. Alternatively, you could put the small measure in a tablespoon to avoid spillage and maybe he will prefer to lick it off. The whole aim of such feeding is to promote the dog into a 'good-doer' which is a dog who, however casually treated, will do well, eats well and requires no special and fancy treatment and thrives all the time. If you have one such as this you are fortunate indeed.

Feeding the adult Cairn

As already intimated, the best quality feeding is in the long run a good investment and a prudent economy. The money expended on good food and attention to feeding generally is likely to offset to quite a considerable degree the outlay for medicines and veterinary bills in the dog's life to come. A sound diet must contain a correct proportion of protein, carbohydrates and fats. Meat, eggs, fish and cheese, etc supply the proteins; cereals, biscuits, bread etc the carbohydrates, while fats are assimilated from the usual sources of milk, butter content, fish oils and the fat on meat, etc. The aim in feeding is to develop and preserve a dog in good health, in good bloom and with an equable and contented frame of mind. The dog's food must therefore be balanced, varied and of the highest standard. With all dogs mealtimes are the important events of the day. Consequently, to give a dog a meal which will benefit him to the full, some careful thought must be applied to the matter.

There is not much extra work involved in conscientious preparation of a dog's meal. Cut up the meat into pieces of manageable size. A dog does not masticate his food in the same way as a human. Most of the break up and dissolving of the food is effected by strong gastric juices in the stomach. Too large lumps of meat might cause choking; pieces which are too small, such as minced meat – perhaps barely suitable for only very young puppies – do not allow the mature animal's gastric juices ample play. Raw, fresh meat is better than cooked, for none of the natural nutriments have been simmered away. Observe scrupulous hygiene with the feeding vessels; dirty plates and dishes harbour disease, and in any case it is only fair and just to the dog to make his meals palatable and well-presented. With most adult dogs, one main meal in the evening, possibly with a few dry biscuits at midday with an adequate drinking water supply available to him all day, constitutes the best form of feeding. Many dogs prefer raw meat and thrive on flesh in this form, but there are good alternatives available in canned form. These are prepared hygienically, and producers are well aware of the valuable market available and ready to meet it with good food, well fortified with minerals and vitamins to meet the special requirements of dogs. A wide range of such canned dog foods is to be seen on retailers' shelves and it is a good idea to let your dog run through a range of the best-known of these to ascertain the kind he favours best. Then you can keep to this brand with only an occasional change for a stand-by in case the popular sort is unavailable one day. The dog will look forward to his dinners and develop a good appetite in advance of them. The same system should apply to biscuits which supply carbohydrates; there being many makes and kinds on the market, not all of them perhaps palatable to individual dogs. A saucer of milk with his biscuits at tea-time will be appreciated, but make sure that the bowl of water already referred to, is near to him at *all* times of the day and night.

It is normally found prudent not to give food to a dog just before retiring, but a small knob of cheese to please him and supply added vitamins will be beneficial. Be careful with bones, the only type permissible are the big shank and marrow bones as these do not splinter and the Cairn Terrier is not endowed with jaws which can do much damage to these although many a youngster will manage to extract the marrow from within some bones, they find it so delectable. Chewing

A trio of Deneland Cairn Terriers, owned by Mr & Mrs P. Towers.

bones does sometimes help a young puppy to loosen unwanted milk teeth although at times a breeder may need to ease out a stubborn canine tooth which if left in would probably cause misplacement of the new and on-coming canine. This, if indeed badly located could well interfere with one of the lines of incisors required to form a desirable level or 'scissor' bite mouth as required by the Standard of the breed. Consequently, a young dog's mouth should be inspected every day while he is making his permanent teeth just in case manual assistance from the owner can prove helpful. Reverting to the gnawing of bones or in fact the chewing of any hard substance which a puppy might engage with, such a habit should be discouraged if the Cairn shows signs of developing an undershot or overshot jaw, for either of these faults would prohibit its owner from winning major prizes under competent judges when the time comes to exhibit his dog. Active bone-biting could well aggravate an already suspect jaw-line.

Teeth

A Cairn Terrier's first teeth (milk teeth) number twenty-eight. These are temporary and are gradually replaced with the teeth which are to be permanent. There are forty-two all told and made up with twelve incisors, four canines, sixteen pre-molars and ten molars. With Cairns, as with some related breeds emanating from the aboriginal Highland Terrier family, it does happen that, depending on the width of the jaw, an odd incisor will be missing, an omission which may not be revealed until full dentition has occurred. It is also possible that a permanent dental complement may lack a molar, but such deficiencies are really no indication of unsoundness in the dog so affected so long as they are minimal and the mouth has full competence in the matters of eating and biting. See also comments on teeth in section on the breed Standard.

Take care with meat which you may be obliged to use for alternative feeding when supplies of normal flesh are difficult to obtain. Knacker's meat comes from an animal which has died; it could be less than fresh before it reaches your dog's feeding bowl and may well be full of veterinary drugs unlikely to do him anything but harm. Offal in the form of ox or sheep hearts is good; ox cheek and ox liver have their uses and values. Tripe and various forms of lower grade offal are perhaps of secondary worth; paunch is recommended by some, but then this may be because it is 'cheap and cheerful'. Nothing has value compared with fresh, raw meat. Steamed white fish, carefully boned is excellent and herrings, when in season, cooked in a pressure cooker, give considerable nourishment.

An adult Cairn Terrier should have at least $\frac{1}{2}$ lb (0.2 kg) fresh raw meat daily. If you are forced to allow him less than this then the balance should be made up with some other form of nourishing food which will maintain him in good bloom and with plenty of vigour.

For the purposes of this section, an adult includes a forward puppy who is at least eight months old. His main meal should be in the evening and concentration should always be on the feeding at this time, given preferably after his exercise or field work. Managed this way, the dog will gain the full nutritive effects of his food while sleeping and his digestion will be of an orderly nature. Always feed a grown Cairn *dry* for soft mushy food is of little use if you aim for best results. Never feed or water after heavy exercise, such as a ratting expedition or other exertions. Let the dog settle down first; get back to normal respiration, then give him a drink, followed by food if a meal time is approaching. A morning meal in the form of cereal and milk or of the type of feeding recommended in the puppy menu section, suitably upped in quantity will prove ideal. Some owners like to give their dogs a drink at night before retiring, but a dog needs to prove his cleanliness overnight to warrant it, and the average owner will know whether a late drink is prudent.

Lastly, for a dog living within the family circle there are often scraps and leftovers for him to consume. It is obvious that some of these, although eaten and enjoyed by humans are totally unsuited to a dog's diet. Take care then that foods likely to purge him are cast elsewhere, especially marinated foods and sauces. Pungent foods will have a particularly bad effect on a Cairn's digestion, so be warned!

Food values

Food provides the body with essential ingredients which enable it to function as Nature intended. A well-balanced menu, as we have emphasised, makes a dog healthy, fit and well and in good mental fettle. It allows the body to grow properly and rectify damage to tissue and also provides energy and correct blood heat. Also, it helps the body to function correctly, keeping it in good working order and protecting it against infection.

The constituents of food fall into four main categories: Proteins, Carbohydrates, Fats and Minerals plus Vitamins which are essential for the regulation of body processes. These are detailed, as follows:

PROTEINS
Important for steady growth and repair of damaged tissue. Sources are mainly meat, poultry, fish, cheese, milk and eggs. They are also

obtainable from cereals, beans, nuts and vegetables. Certain root vegetables and the edible seeds of some leguminous plants have their value.

CARBOHYDRATES (STARCH)
These give energy. They are contained in foods such as maize, flour, bread, biscuits, honey, sugars, conserves and sweets, also some root vegetables. Surplus carbohydrate starch is converted to fats and stored in the body.

FATS
These give energy also by combustion with the tissues, but any surplus to immediate needs is stored in the body. Sources are fat meats, butter, margarine, lard, suet, vegetable oils, oily fish, milk, cream, cheese and eggs. When meat or milk are absent from the diet cod-liver oil is a suitable substitute owing to its Vitamin A and D content.

VITAMINS
These are a group of organic substances, essential (in small quantities) for the normal functioning of metabolism in the body. They occur naturally in certain foods and much has been learnt in the last few decades to feature their worth. Here they are dealt with briefly. Some are manufactured in the body itself, others are supplied by diet.

Vitamin-A This keeps the glands, teeth and dentition healthy. It is important for development of bone, normal growth, eyesight and the prevention of night-blindness and the protection of animal cellular tissue from disease and the body from infection. The following sources are rich in this Vitamin: Halibut- and Cod-liver oils, fish liver and roes, mackerel and herring, milk, eggs, honey, maize meal, turnip tops, tomatoes, carrots, watercress, spinach, dried fruits, liver, kidney and lean meat.

Vitamin-B complex Excellent for maintaining a good standard of the nervous system; it occurs especially in liver and brewers' yeast, cereals, oatmeal, offal, fish, onions, wheat germ oil, rabbit, nuts, soya beans, garlic, lean pork. It is very important to health.

Vitamin-C This is ideal for keeping skin and coat in good order and is another aid to teeth condition. It is obtained from citric fruit juices (ascorbic acid) and certain vegetables. Sources include oranges, blackcurrants, haws, parsnips, celery, carrots, leeks, mackerel, heart and liver; used to cure scurvy long before vitamins were 'discovered'.

Vitamin-D This is noted particularly for preventing rickets and it is an important factor in maintaining growth and bone development. Without it, vital minerals like calcium and phosphorus cannot be absorbed. Main sources of this Vitamin are animal oils and fats, but sunshine and ultra-violet rays play a large part in producing this Vitamin, which is why it is often termed the 'sunshine' Vitamin. Can be absorbed through the skin.

Vitamin-E This is termed the anti-sterility Vitamin, another name for tocopherol and is believed vital in the work of a breeding kennel by having an important bearing on fertility in the dog and bitch. An active stud dog can manage well at his job if he has been reared from puppyhood on Vitamin-E for it will maintain his potency and delay advance of possible sterility. When given to the bitch, the possible chances of dead puppies or absorbed foetuses during pregnancy will be brought to a minimum. The most useful source of this Vitamin is wheat-germ oil in the form of capsules also Vitamin-E Succinate, both of which make dosing easy. It should be remembered however that fish, liver, barley, honey and green vegetables like spinach all have their values in this Vitamin, whose total worth and effectiveness is not entirely established.

MINERALS
There is a huge selection of proprietary mineral and vitamin products on the market these days, many of them aimed at the dog breeder and owner. Minerals help in growth and body protection and control body processes.

Calcium is necessary for the health of heart, nerves, blood and muscles. It helps formation of teeth and bone structure. It comes mainly from milk, cheese, shredded raw green vegetables, fish and all flours except wholemeal.

Iron is needed for the formation of red blood cells and the rectification of an anaemic condition. There are iron tonics on the market suitable for the dog, and it is worthwhile enquiring from a reputable pet shop or your veterinary surgeon for a recommended brand. Natural sources of iron include green vegetables, meat, egg yolk and maize, also liver and kidney.

Sodium is found in common salt compounds and is essential to body health, where a balance is needed between potassium and sodium, salts used extensively in medicine.

Iodine is essential for efficient function of glands and tissue. It is to be found in water, both tap and from the sea, also it is to be extracted from some seaweeds.

Water itself must not be forgotten for this is necessary for passing through the body waste and food products, also heat in the normal functioning of the dog's system.

Note: Both Vitamins A and D are fat soluble and both are dangerous if given in excess. The two Vitamins are associated with each other in egg yolk, fish oils (notably sardines) rich in Vitamin-D especially, also milk, butter and margarine. By feeding foods associated and well-fortified with Vitamin-D and giving doses of foods containing Vitamin-A there exists a danger of administering a harmful amount.

Training

The true Cairn Terrier is an active, inquisitive and athletic member of the Terrier family. He is fully endowed with superior canine intelligence and determination. Such a fine temperament needs moulding while in the course of his development. This is why most owners prefer a small puppy to an adult, for the former can be trained much easier and to its owner's specific requirements. Firm training is essential; unfortunately, a lot of owners fail to apply rules and regulations to their dogs until too late. Many seem to think that a small puppy rushing pell-mell about the house, knocking down this, ruining that, constitutes a comic circus turn for the family circle to enjoy. It might well be for a short time, but only while the puppy is very small – it becomes far from funny when the dog is mature and remains untrained and undisciplined. Then he becomes a nuisance to himself and others and an embarrassment and probable expense to his owner.

The first year of a dog's existence is of major importance, this being the period when a puppy is most impressionable and normally easily trained. Unless an owner is prepared to undertake the responsibility of training and regulating his dog he should not buy one. A poorly trained dog reflects upon his owner's aptitude as a trainer. The first word a young dog must learn is 'No!'. It is an easy word to say and easy for a dog to understand its implication. It is true also that most puppies are willing and eager to learn it. Never, never, thrash a puppy if he is slow to learn. This is a fatal move in training any animal. Not many dogs ever regain confidence in the person who beat them, quite apart from the fact that a beaten dog will seldom respond properly thereafter. Corporal punish-

Ferelith Hamilton (Mrs Stafford Somerfield) Editor-in-Chief *Dog World* with her Oudenarde Crest of Gold. (*Fall*)

ment, when it has to be applied, is better administered very lightly with a rolled-up newspaper. Dogs dislike the rustling impact of this discipline which should be used with the word 'No!' when it seems deserved. In a very short time, it will become quite unnecessary to bring it into use – the word of command itself will suffice or even the mere showing of the newspaper will do the trick. The puppy may hate it, but he is unlikely to bear any malice about it. By this simple and humane method, a youngster can be gently persuaded to stop biting furniture, nibbling ankles and to lie down and stop making a nuisance of himself. Just show him what to do in the simplest, most commonsense method adaptable to the problem and he will learn quite quickly. When only one dog is kept it is easier for the trainer and the pupil has the advantage of personal attention. When there is a number of youngsters in course of training, each one should have just as much individual training applied gradually and in a gentle but firm manner. It is important that repetition of the routine should be applied daily and it is often a good idea to allocate a certain hour of the day for such training.

HOUSE-TRAINING

Training a small puppy to be clean in the home has always been a problem for the new owner; even a deterrent to dog ownership for some house-proud people. It need never be, for it is simple to house-break a puppy in a very short time. Puppies of just two months of age sleep a great deal, just like babies. They should be allowed to do this as often as they wish and children should be taught never to disturb them while they rest. Quite apart from a small dog requiring ample sleep to store up energy, even the mildest mannered dog must be hard put to it to retain good humour when pummelled suddenly out of a deep sleep.

When a puppy has had enough sleep he will open his eyes; as soon as the eyes are open he will want to urinate. That is a cardinal certainty and it is the pattern to watch for, as at that point he should be taken up or guided either to the garden door or to his sand or newspaper-lined tray. If it is to be out of doors and the weather is sufficiently clement, the door should be closed on him. Watch him until he has squatted and completed the job. Then open the door and let him in – but not before he has relieved himself, however much he might be complaining at being shut out. If he has to use a sand or dirt tray, then keep him within the perimeter of the tray until he has finished, then ceremoniously (almost), lift him off. A few lessons such as this will find the idea well embedded in his mind and before long, the instant he opens his eyes from a sleep he will move to terrain beyond the garden door or to the sand tray and do his business. Be sure to praise and pet him when he is good and only the mildest scold when he is not, for he is bound to make one or two mistakes while learning. Never scold him when he makes one or two puddles indoors because the door to the 'ablutions' was not opened fast enough to let him get out when nature was calling urgently. To punish him for something which is really the owner's fault is patently unfair and may well cause a set-back in his training.

It is probable that he will forget himself at night in any case. Small puppies are continually making puddles – their bladders are quite weak at two or even three months of age. The best plan, apart from making a prudent point of giving him minimal liquid at night before retiring, is to cover the floor of his pen, or the kitchen where he sleeps, with newspapers. Then, in the morning, these can be gathered up and put into the disposal bin without fuss. While the youngster is learning to be clean it would be foolish in the extreme to leave him in rooms where there are valuable carpets and curtains. Any untrained animal should be kept where he can do no damage to property and fitments. If a puppy tears up one's best carpet slippers or rips open a cushion or two, never blame the pup; it is the fault of the person who left them there unattended with such lovely temptations!

ON THE LEAD

The next step is to get the young dog used to collar and lead. Naturally, he should not be taken on the sidewalk and the streets until he has had all his inoculations. Too many health hazards exist where older dogs have paraded. Lamp-posts especially seem to harbour diseases, yet they hold a traditional fascination for dogs of all ages. For this reason, it is best to give the puppy his elementary lead training in the home and garden.

A cheap collar should be purchased initially for he will soon grow out of his first collar and it will have to be discarded. Buy a light-weight, narrow strap-like collar with lead to match. The youngster should be trained to accept this collar by putting it on for short periods during the day, then progressively longer periods, until he finally accepts it. At first, he will probably scratch at it with some irritation and annoyance, but eventually it will be tolerated all day with little or no fuss. By wearing a collar he will become more manageable, but it should be removed at night while he sleeps as if left on it may disarrange the hairline round his neck, causing an unsightly ruff.

Later, when the puppy finds the collar comfortable and to his taste, a light lead can be attached to it and he can be encouraged to walk up and down. He will not like the idea very much and will probably emulate a captured trout on the end of a line. However, with some reassurance, coupled with patience from the owner, he will learn to move composedly back and forth. Do not forget to use a tit-bit or two in the course of this training, giving him one every time he behaves well. Watch for the puppy which pulls excessively and tries to dash too far ahead of his trainer or handler. Too much of this will detract from the correct development of his shoulders, quite apart from the annoyance such behaviour will cause his trainer. Keep early training to periods of about ten minutes' duration to save the puppy getting bored. If he pulls too much tap him lightly across the muzzle with your rolled-up newspaper, giving the command 'Heel' or 'Back'. He will soon learn not to pull. A puppy which on the other hand drags back, squats in a stubborn fashion and digs his feet into the ground, so to speak, has to be encouraged forward with tasty morsels, plus a determined pull forward on the lead which should bring him into mobility. With puppies destined for the show ring, it is wise to train them to move on either side of the handler, but when obedience work is the aim, then always keep the pupil on the handler's *left* side. Strive always for good presentation when your dog walks besides you; although with collar and lead, he should look free, easy and confident in his movement, quite independent of his handler and appear free from manual control.

Exercise

A healthy Cairn Terrier needs a lot of exercise. He is quite capable of doing six times and more the amount that his equally healthy owner would normally seek to do and still be ready for more. Make sure he is never let off the lead where traffic is a hazard. Even the best trained ones sometimes fall foul of fast cars. The open fields and parks are best for free running off the lead. In such confines a ball game can be held without much fear that the dog will come into trouble. Watch should be kept for other dogs, of course, making sure that no mischief is made either by him or against him. Lakesides are probably best kept clear of, for Cairns enjoy a swim but this does make for wet dogs in the car and it is not unusual for a dog to encounter stagnant water which might endanger his health. A dog being conditioned for show work needs to be in good firm order. Walk him several miles a day, if you can. Take him over rough ground, even cinder tracks are good for they will harden his pads and feet, and strengthen the pasterns, quite apart from giving benefit to the hindquarters. Keep an eye open for hills and slopes. Throw the ball up their inclines and let the dog retrieve it. The 'push' he has to give his hindquarters to get to the top will greatly develop his hind muscles and at the same time trim down to the minimum his toe-nails. Although free-running exercise is good for him, make sure that he gets plenty of exercise on the lead. It maintains steadiness and rhythm of gait and this develops an elegant deportment which will hold the dog in good stead when he enters the show ring. The lead from owner's hand to dog's collar should be slack never taut. The lead should be used to impart instructive pressures. A natural action must be encouraged and then you may be sure your dog will enjoy his perambulations and so will you.

Never over-walk a young puppy for this can do irreparable harm. Exercise is the second most important need to a Cairn – the first being food, of course. Therefore, when it is pouring with rain outside, do not be tempted to deprive him of his daily walk, however put-off you may be at the thought of getting wet. Take him out and when you return make sure he is dried down well and towelled properly underneath – then he will come to no harm. No one should buy a dog unless he intends to maintain that dog's fitness by feeding the animal and giving it ample and regular exercise.

A fat Cairn is neither a delight to look at, nor does he enjoy life. A dog gets best results from his exercise when he is walked alone, but obviously someone owning a number of dogs cannot do this and will need help when exercising. Always be aware that one dog will get another into trouble; it being a fact that once you have two, you have the nucleus of a pack! If a dog or dogs are walked in public the handler must know that he is in control should an emergency arise. One sometimes sees a juvenile out with a fine adult Cairn; this is wrong, an adult should be at the other end of the lead, so that the dog is under complete control as all dogs should be when they are on the public highway. Indoors, it is a different matter for temptation capable of precipitating a serious incident is unlikely to arise.

Guarding the home

The Cairn Terrier is not so much a physical guard as a competent watchdog. His size and weight are such that he cannot throw much armament against a human intruder. However, he is a natural watchdog and persistent in his mode of warning. He will bark vociferously at most things which distract him – other creatures and unexpected noises. He seldom barks without cause at the outset, but sometimes he does not know when to stop! Such enthusiasm needs to be directly under an owner's training scheme and the dog must be praised for his efforts at giving the alarm, but stopped from barking continuously for no apparent reason.

If a puppy is a little slow at showing guarding ability, he can be encouraged in the following way. The owner will have to put in some 'acting' to achieve good results. Get someone outside the house to ring the bell or knock on the door or window. The average puppy will at once cock an ear and listen – he is at once surprised and aware. At this point, if the puppy does not bark himself, the owner should do his best imitation of a bark – 'Woof' or something similar. No matter how foolish he may feel in delivering this doggy sound, he should come in again with another 'Woof', the more menacing and intense the impersonation it is, the better. The puppy will probably catch on to this after a few tries and before long as soon as the bell rings or the knocker is assaulted he will 'Woof' too! Once he has started to bark, he will get enthusiastic, especially if encouraged and the lesson will soon sink in; certainly such lessons are seldom forgotten.

Bathing

A Cairn Terrier does not need much or any bathing. Of course if he has encountered some obnoxious substance which makes close proximity to the dog unpleasant or if he has become covered in mud, then it is essential. A small puppy should never be bathed unless there is a specific reason and care should be taken that the bathing is not too energetic as the youngster will be frightened. When bathing a Cairn, ensure that the water is just warm. An over-hot bath will upset any dog and make him quite uncooperative next time you want to put him in the tub. He should not have been fed for at least three hours prior to the event and certainly given a chance to relieve himself first. The wise owner will have made sure that everything he needs for the dog's bath is close to hand. The items needed are two rough Turkish terry towels, one to soak off the initial moisture, the other to remove the dampness and to completely dry underneath the dog and around his most tender parts. If you can arrange the positioning of the bath where he will have a chance to shake himself, so much the better for then you will soak the towels much less.

A good dog shampoo can be used and there are a number of reliable makes to choose from. Follow the instructions for its use, but make sure you remove every vestige of it when time comes round for rinsing the dog. If you fail to do this, the coat may get clogged and matted, causing the dog some discomfort and irritation. Extra care should be given when bringing the shampoo near to the dog's eyes and ears. Some owners smear a little petroleum jelly around the eyes and insert a jelly-smeared wad of cotton wool into the dog's ears for safety. It seems almost unnecessary to warn owners that all such grease applications and wads *must* be disposed of when the bath is over. It is vital that the dog is dried off completely. The parts to heed particularly are the soft-flesh areas of the underparts and genitals and around the loins too, also between the toes. Let the dog remain in an even temperature for a while – on no account let him out of doors too soon. It should be noted that an adverse effect can be given to a Cairn's coat with too much rubbing. This will remove some of the natural oils so important to the harsh feel required of the coat. Some breeders use a hair dryer to complete drying, after initial work with a towel. The coat should be groomed into shape as you progress and not allowed to twist and curl.

Grooming

The healthy Cairn in good bloom needs very little grooming. This is a great advantage with this breed which has always been a 'natural' one. All the dog really needs is the daily application of brush and comb.

However, first stand your subject on a level where you can survey him in detail. Then, you can examine him properly and inspect every part of his body to ensure he is in good shape. Dogs sometimes get tears and scratches while going about their daily travels and these should receive attention to ensure no complications develop. In Spring and Summer grass seeds and ticks are prevalent. The former get in and on the dog's coat and need to be removed manually; the ticks, common in sheep country, are a nuisance because they grip the animal's flesh and are not easy to dislodge. They can be removed by dropping a spot of Eucalyptus Oil or Turpentine on them and they will fall off. Lice and fleas sometimes use a dog as host and these can be found sheltering beneath his tail, along the spine and often around the ears. Dusting with a good DDT de-lousing powder has good effect, although some people prefer to give a course of anti-parasite baths which is very effective. Look at the eyes and any foreign bodies and discharge evident should be wiped away with a soft tissue or cotton wool. Look in between the toes and remove any tar or chemicals which may adhere there.

For the actual grooming you will require the following 'tools': two metal combs, one with wide open teeth, the other with close teeth. Also, a brush of a kind freely available in pet shops. This is a double-sided brush, one side bristle the other side a wire brush with metal tines well spaced and designed to draw out loose hair and open up the dog's coat. Use the open teeth comb all over the body, running it from above the eyes, the brow, occipital region, neck, withers and back right down to the tail. Then bring in the double-sided brush, giving the dog a good brisk going-over and removing any semblance of tangle while disposing of dead hairs and coat castings. The close-toothed comb must be used for grooming the legs and feet and to clean-up loose undercoat hair to make way for new growth. Any sections in the coat and particularly around the ears which have become cloyed or felted can be dealt with by kneading in a little olive oil or similar penetrant which will soon solve the problem and loosen up the matting.

As stated at the start of this section the Cairn needs the least of grooming, the only two places where attention is sometimes needed with a trimming knife being at the back of the forelegs and the feather at the back of and below the tail. Superfluous hair can be removed by hand or by light application of a trimming knife, but these are the only two places that any self-respecting breeder and groom would approach with a knife.

Teeth should be examined; the Cairn's teeth are big, white and strong and they must be maintained this way. Remove tartar sediment with a tooth scaler and brush the teeth with a soft tooth brush, using a TCP solution (1 in 10) or a half and half solution of hydrogen peroxide and water. Nails are a different story; not many breeders care to tackle long nails on a dog for fear of clipping too near to the quick. It can be a tricky job and most owners prefer to use a veterinary surgeon. However, if your dog has had plenty of road work and not too much running around on soft ground it is likely that the nails will be at the right length.

Fighting

The average Cairn does not go around looking for trouble, but he is not backward when it comes to answering an insult from another canine or in an effort to protect some member of his family circle. If the dog is running with his collar on, it is an easy job to lift him up and providing he has no secure hold he will usually break off the fight. If he is well held on to his adversary, you might try to prise his jaw open and remove him, but owners who do this sometimes get bitten inadvertently. It is better to slide your right hand under his collar, knuckles down, twist the collar and push the biter into the bitten one. The former will not be able to breathe and will open his mouth to come up for air; then you can remove him. Less determined fighting pairs can be separated by the more traditional method of throwing a bucket of water over them! If both participants are your own two, it is important to bring them together in a reassuring atmosphere as soon as possible. It is a nuisance if they should nurse a permanent enmity towards each other which would necessitate separate kennelling and an ever-watchful eye during exercising. If you have a goodly number of Cairns running free and a fight starts with the pack involved then you have what is called in the Midlands a 'battle royal'. This presents a problem for a solitary person. However, start with one of them, the most determined, grab him or her and remove from the scene. Come back and go through the melée removing one at a time until you end up with a fighting pair which you will have to deal with as suggested above. Make sure there are no wounds which need treatment is the final task, after such an exciting interlude!

Elementary obedience

It is never too early to commence training a Cairn Terrier. At eight weeks of age, a good deal of sense exists in that unique headpiece. The average puppy is anxious to learn that he can relate well with his owner. The master will get pleasure in owning a dog which will do what he is told and the dog will enjoy himself better because he knows that he has pleased his master. Training such a small puppy must inevitably be of the gradual kind. A puppy over-worked in the scheme of training becomes stale and bored with it all; such a youngster seldom becomes a successful pupil. Not more than ten minutes at a time should be devoted to training a puppy. At all times he should be treated kindly, intelligently and with common sense. The occasional tit-bit reward for good results is essential and this should be accompanied with a pat on the head and a few words of praise.

The following exercises are recommended for the welfare of the *pet* Cairn Terrier, making him a welcome member of the family circle, knowing how to behave and how to become unobtrusive when required to by his master. If he shows exceptional prowess at obedience work, then he might even be considered for advanced courses at a later date. He would then be allowed to enter obedience tests which are held by some canine societies in conjunction with their own dog-show events. There are also registered training clubs which hold Obedience Dog

Shows under Kennel Club rules, and although such bodies aim at standards demanding high canine intelligence, there is no reason at all why the average Cairn Terrier cannot achieve top honours in this fascinating pursuit and hobby.

'COME' WHEN CALLED

This is a lesson which every dog must learn. Any Cairn who does not know or refuses to come when called is an embarrassment, even a liability to his owner as well as being an unhappy dog in the bargain. It is always best to start training with the pupil hungry. He will then be more appreciative of the tit-bit rewards which can be won for achievement. The lesson can be arranged with either one tutor, or two. It is probably taught quicker and more effectively with two. Let one person hold the youngster and the other at, say, ten yards distance, call it by name, gently adding 'Come!'. The puppy will probably move at once to the caller, who should praise him, pat him and award a tasty morsel. This move should then be followed by the same procedure from the helper calling 'Come!'. When the puppy has gone away at the second call, he will get another word of praise, another tit-bit for his good work.

This formula repeated a dozen times or more from one person to the other and back again will soon sink into the youngster's consciousness. It should then be tried by one of the instructors when the puppy is travelling half-way back to the other. He should call 'Come!' and if the puppy turns around in his tracks and returns, then the praise should be lavish indeed and the tit-bit an extra good one. Should he not track back and merely continue to the other person, then he must not be rewarded or praised. Perhaps this will confuse him initially, but he will soon learn after a few more examples. It is best to give at least a dozen lessons to each movement, and to repeat for three consecutive days allowing ample time for the lesson to be learnt.

It is normal to give initial instruction in the precincts of the home or kennel. Not so many distractions exist there as out of doors, so the puppy will learn quicker. However, it is more important for the training to have good effect away from the youngster's usual haunts and as soon as he seems ready for the final phase of this lesson he should be taken to a local park or field. Tie a training cord, which can be twenty feet long to his collar and hold the other end. Release him and puppy-like he will make a bee-line for some interesting object – a tree, a pond or another dog. As he nears the end of the now running-out cord which you hold, call 'Come!'. It is likely in his excitement that he will be quite heedless of the command and run on, only to be turned head over heels when the cord reaches its extremity. This sudden upset will prove an unpleasant surprise, but it will make him think. After it has been repeated a few times he will halt in his rush as soon as he hears you call 'Come!'. Soon, remembering his starting lesson with this command he will turn around and walk back to you. This will prove the lesson learnt and following a few more tests to ensure that it has 'sunk in', the next simple lesson can be taught.

'SIT'
With official obedience training in mind, a dog should always be taught to sit on the handler's left side, hard by the handler's heels when he halts. He should be walked on a slack lead, his body close by the holder's left leg. A tit-bit held in the hand will keep his attention rapt and he will not pull away or be distracted. With the command 'Sit!' the handler will halt suddenly in his tracks, at the same time swinging his body round to the left without moving his feet. As this is done, the dog should automatically sit. If he carries on walking, snap the lead back from your stationary position, making the dog sit back on his haunches. When he does this, either naturally, or forced by the snap-back method, he should be praised and patted. This will encourage him to do it again. If difficulty is experienced in achieving a sitting position, the dog can be persuaded by taking his collar in the right hand, pulling back a little and

Woodthorpe Puck and Ch. Woodthorpe Madcap, owned by Miss M. Morgan. (*Fall*)

at the same time (with the left hand) pressing him down into a sit. If it is found that when he learns to sit on command he sits rather wide of your left leg you might feel inclined to move sideways towards him. This is wrong – you should move *away* from him even more. Then you should encourage him to narrow the gap with your left hand and some cajolery.

'DOWN'

This exercise can be usefully employed as part two of the 'Sit' lesson. Thus, when you have a dog fully taught to obey that command, it is already half-way towards the completion of the 'Down' lesson. The best method is again with the pupil on the trainer's left side and the lead under his left foot, its end held high in his right hand. As the command 'Down!' is given in a firm tone, the lead is pulled with the right hand. This will cause the dog to be pressed down from the neck end, while with your left hand you can press down on his rear section.

'STAY'

An important exercise and for simplicity in training, it is best to let the exercise follow the dog's mastery of the 'Down' position. This is because it is the most relaxed position the pupil can hold if he is to be in one position for any length of time. Having given the command 'Down!' and this being obeyed, the trainer should now stand in front of him – you can point to the spot where he has 'downed' if you wish to add emphasis to the command 'Stay!', as you move back one step. If the dog is restless and gets up to follow you, get him immediately into the 'Down' position. Try again, and eventually he will understand that he has to remain there even with a number of yards between you. It is best to make the initial practice still holding his lead. This will allow you to step back a few paces; a check cord will be useful over a longer distance if you want to play for safety. Soon, you will be able to disappear from the dog's view while he remains in the 'Stay' position.

'HEEL'

This is really no more than basic lead training, which has already been covered in the appropriate section. However, it should be remembered that the command 'Heel!' is a useful one and which appears readily understood by the dog. With the dog on the left side, the lead held in the trainer's right hand, a slack loop should be maintained under the dog's neck; in effect, there should be no tautness or tension in the lead. Dog and trainer should start off together with the command 'Heel!'. The speed of the movement should be gauged so that the lead remains slack and the dog is hard by the trainer's left heel at all times. Give the pupil plenty of praise for good results and an occasional tit-bit. Later, when he is adept, he can be tried without the restrictive confinement of the lead. This is the 'heel free' exercise. If he does not appear ready for this at first attempt he should be put back on the lead and given further training.

Points to remember include the importance of ensuring that the pupil has complete confidence in his tutor; for this reason, make sure that the dog is not scolded unnecessarily. A violent show of impatience on your part can set back many hours of progress. If you make a mistake with any instruction put it right immediately, and, if the dog seems confused make a fuss of him. If the dog fails to perform satisfactorily in an exercise which he has done previously with perfection, do not let him get away with it. Get him back to the task at once and you will probably find he does it perfectly. Dogs are quick to take advantage and any slackness condoned while training can delay progress. Always watch for individual reactions in pupils. A method used to train one dog might prove totally unsuited to another. If this should be noted never use it if the pupil seems to find it unpleasant, or fails to learn from its application.

Car travel

Always get a dog used to car travel or public transport right from puppyhood. Once he has had all his inoculations he can be taken out in a car either before his meal or at least two hours after it, the reason being that he is not so easily induced to actual sickness. With a full stomach before a journey a dog will suffer nausea and either slobber or vomit within a short time of starting off. It is usually those dogs who have been sick in a car who think they are going to be sick every time they enter a car thereafter. Providing the puppy can have a few consecutive trips without being sick he is unlikely to experience nausea in future outings.

It is important, therefore, to try and avoid sickness on his first car journey. The best way to do this is to have a companion with you who will take the puppy on his lap. The initial run out should be one of short duration. If the puppy looks uncomfortable and begins to open and close his jaws, it is a sign that he feels sick. Stop the car until he has settled down or carry him back home. It will be found that the car trips can be increased in mileage each time out until quite a lengthy trip can be made without the dog feeling ill. By this time there is a good chance that he will have been cured of the weakness.

For chronic cases of car sickness there are effective drug remedies on the market which your veterinary surgeon should be asked to prescribe for a Cairn Terrier, according to the age of the subject.

Ch. Ribbledene Dinah,
Rambler of Woolgreaves
and Ch. Merry Man Max,
owned by Mrs M.
Greaves. (*Fall*)

Needless noise

Some Cairn Terriers like to make their presence known and occasionally one encounters a puppy which barks or howls so incessantly as to constitute a nuisance to owner and neighbours alike. Small puppies cannot understand why they should not make a noise, so the best method of correction has to be largely psychological. The youngster must be made to learn that every time he opens his mouth to bark or scream for no reason at all, that something unpleasant happens! When he realises this, he will think twice before he starts up again for fear that it will trigger off the 'treatment'.

An effective training method is to wait quietly outside the door of the room where he is kept. As soon as he howls or barks without reason, burst open the door and shout 'No!' or 'Quiet!'. Taken by surprise he will probably gape at you and stop his noise. Then you retire from him and wait outside, waiting for the next howl to start up. Almost before you hear it leave his mouth, be in there with the shout of 'No!' or

'Quiet!'. The youngster will not like this at all and even less if the admonition is accompanied with a sharp disciplinary tap. After a few sessions of this double-act performance, the puppy will usually give it up as a bad job.

Unless the pupil is quite stupid, of course, he will learn quickly not to be so vociferous and it is important that he does, for this is a bad habit in a dog and a great patience tester. A danger exists, as the reader will realise, that a puppy which has been trained out of needless barking may not bark a valid warning when required to do so, such as when a fire breaks out or an intruder is heard and threatens. However, a Cairn is well-endowed with sense and will know when his vocal services are required to guard his home and himself, so no worry should be expended on this point. In any case, training bad habits out of a puppy normally does the growing-up Cairn a favour and does not destroy his natural attributes.

Jumping up

Few canine habits annoy as much as the one which makes a dog bound straight out of a muddy garden puddle directly into the lap of a guest. New clothes are ruined and suits and dresses bespattered with filth and mud! Such a dog reflects at once on his owner's aptitude as a trainer. Clearly, such an irritating habit as this must be broken. Obviously, the first thing is to ensure that at all times muddy dogs must not encounter guests, but even the best laid plans sometimes go wrong and it is as well to prepare some corrective remedy for the next incident.

Patently, the jumper must be pushed quite forcefully away from his target as he leaps. Shout 'Down!' or 'No!' at him – very loudly, if it is in any way to prove effective, for the boisterous dog hears very little when he is excited and he needs to be halted in his tracks. Assuming that he is making a mark for you and if he ignores your command and is scrambling around your shoes ready to jump, press down with your foot firmly on to his back paws as you give the command. This is done with only light pressure, of course, but he will note its discomfort. If he persists in jumping, bring one knee up and let him bounce and bound against that. It will almost certainly topple him over backwards and he will find this most unpleasant. A few lessons of this sort are calculated to quieten him down and mend his jumping ways.

Kennels

One Cairn Terrier is better kept in the house, although being such a small breed you might extend to several if you can manage them.

However, it amounts to the fact that a dog kept out of doors in a kennel is not much use to anyone, except as a breeding proposition. Such a dog becomes bored, often lacks affinity with his owner and is quite capable of ignoring any intruder. Further, he may well suffer in the development of his intelligence, whereas the indoor dog seems to know everything that is said to him! However, when a number of dogs are kept and are engaged in running a proper breeding kennel, the situation is different. Kennel life for the dogs becomes essential, and there are a number of comfortable models in pre-fabricated kennels to be bought these days by mail order and from local sources.

Great care must be taken to pick the right sort of structure and to ensure that it will provide a happy and comfortable home for the dogs and still allow strict hygiene. The kennel site should not be erected under trees, although a screen of trees protecting it from the prevailing winds of the locality is often to be desired. It should stand on well-drained sandy soil or gravel, preferably facing south or south-west. A range of four adjoining kennels is a nice start for a novice, with a compartment at one end to house brushes, brooms, shovel, sawdust and disinfectant supplies with easy access. The cautious breeder might well consider a further single kennel placed well away from the rest to be used as a sick bay in an emergency requiring isolation.

Most kennels are insufficiently high. This means that the breeder has to spend a considerable time in them in a hunched-up position. This is neither good for one's back nor for efficiency in cleaning and the management of stock. It is best to allow at least 6 feet (1.8 metres) from floor to roof so that most people can stand inside comfortably. Each resident Cairn should have a floor space of about 97 square feet (9 square metres), at least, especially if heating is to be installed. With no heating arrangements, then too much individual space is not a good thing in winter, for the Cairn may be hard put to it to radiate enough body warmth to keep himself cosy in spite of his wonderful double coat. There should be a run of at least 8 feet (2½ metres) long to every kennel, bounded on both sides and front. It is better to have the sides partitioned to minimise stand-up barking between the inmates, but the front should be of chain link so the dogs can survey the scene and be supervised themselves. Height of sides and front should be about 6 feet (1.8 metres). If you have a regular 'escaper' top his run with perspex or similar, although the height of run planned above should keep him inside.

Each kennel should have a sleeping bench which will slide out easily for simple cleaning and which will keep the inmate free from draughts which can debilitate, even kill a dog. It is also a good idea to improvise a ventilation system which can be adjusted to suit outside weather conditions.

If finance permits, try to construct doors from the run into the outside world on the 'inner chamber' system. This means two doors in use – the outside one you open to enter, then close it with yourself inside. You then open the second door to enter the actual run, safe in the knowledge that the dog within cannot slip past you and escape. Kennel hygiene is vital and this should receive daily attention, going into every corner with a mild, then stronger, solution for swabbing down the outside concrete runs. 'Dettol' is a well-tried and trusted antiseptic germicide for this job, not only that, but it can be used for bathing cuts, bites, abrasions and stings, when prepared in the form of a suitable solution.

An alternative form of run covering to concrete, which perhaps is inclined to retain excess moisture after rain (unless it is sloped down away from the kennel) and also hold the heat in summer, is prepared with a foundation of coarse clinker topped with a layer of gravel or screened cinders. The whole should be well firmed and most important, it should be set over well-drained ground.

Lastly, try and keep the kennel buildings within comfortable distance from the house with a suitable paved way leading to it. The dogs will appreciate being near to human activities and you will appreciate only a short walk with dry access on your journeys to and fro.

6 Exhibiting

Not many people enter the dog show 'game' of their own volition. They are frequently coerced into making an entry at the local canine society's event by some person, who, seeing them with an attractive Cairn Terrier youngster, accosts them and informs them that the specimen is a good one and ought to be shown. Most owners are naturally proud of their pedigree Cairns and it takes very little encouragement to persuade them to try their luck. Probably knowing next to nothing about the finer points of the breed, let alone the official breed Standard, they hope merely that the dog will win a prize. Their attitude is as if they were buying a raffle ticket! On the other hand, they do not care much if the dog wins nothing. In fact, the whole venture is treated like a game – which of course, it is at this early stage. Unfortunately, at times, a different aspect arises – their dog, perhaps an average one, either by virtue of the fact that it has had no or only poor competition at the show or has been before an incompetent adjudicator, wins a major prize. Perhaps other Cairn people present flatter the dog and his owner becomes over-ambitious for him. At times like this there is a danger that the dog-show 'bug' will bite hard. Then, the simple recreation of exhibiting can become less of a pastime and more of a business, highly competitive and well spiced with deadly rivalries and jealousies.

Chs. Merrymeet Medea, Merrymeet Diana, Merrymeet Cornelian, owned by Mrs E. F. Leverton. (*Fall*)

Let it be said at once that dog-showing is a good hobby. It is the shop window of the dog world and develops a keen and healthy competitive spirit among its devotees. To some, concerned largely with the commercial possibilities and potentialities of the Cairn world, it opens up lucrative horizons. The breed is in great demand these days having risen well up the Terrier popularity chart in recent years. Good prices are procured for puppies at home and abroad. However, most people who commence exhibiting are more concerned with getting expert opinion from the various judges on their dogs. Later, they will wish to breed from their bitches, hoping to produce outstanding Cairn Terriers from their planned litters. Perhaps, even to be lucky enough to produce a home-bred champion. Also, later on, they will strive for premier show awards to improve, even perpetuate, their kennel names. Certainly, in the course of their career they will meet a lot of nice people, make some real and lasting friends and enjoy the social side which exists so warmly in dogdom.

Ch. Impstown Jenny Geddes, owned by Miss J. Hall. (*Anne Roslin-Williams*)

Picking the show

Both the weekly journals devoted to dogs, *Dog World* and *Our Dogs*, publish dog show announcements in their columns. Here, the intending exhibitor will find details of shows to be held in the near future. The various types of shows, i.e. Exemption, Sanction, Limited, Open and Championship events, will be represented, and once a year the great Kennel Club Cruft's Dog Show will be announced in plenty of time for eligible exhibitors to make their plans. All these will offer a good selection for the enthusiast. The procedure is to write or telephone the honorary secretary or show manager of the society concerned and request a schedule of the classification offered. The show might be for Cairn Terriers only, in which case it would be a special breed club event, and of particular interest to the average Cairn owner. Alternatively, it may be that many different breeds are to be shown and it is then called an 'All Breeds' or 'Any Variety event'. Both types of show have their useful features, although it is probably best to enter at shows where only Cairns make the competition. Such a show would be run by one of the specialist societies (*see*: Appendix 1) and the judge appointed would be a Cairn expert. This means that every Cairn would be judged competently by a specialist and one would possibly get a more detailed opinion of an exhibit from such a judge. In any case, all such shows should receive maximum support from breed lovers, for that helps to get them perpetuated. It is wise also to show the dog under a number of experienced all-rounders (judges who have knowlege of all breeds) in order to test the dog's chances to win in any type of competition.

Types of show

EXEMPTION SHOWS

The Kennel Club licences a number of different kind of shows. The most 'junior' form is the Exemption Show. A dog can be entered at such an event even if not registered at the Kennel Club. Neither do the usual Kennel Club Rules apply, except that most of the disciplinary rules have to be observed. For pedigree dogs only four classes are permitted where they can be judged according to their various breed points and standards. Such classes have to be of a general nature; 'Any Variety Open', 'Any Variety Sporting' being two examples. It is usual and popular to arrange the remaining classes so that pedigree dogs, cross-breeds and mongrels can compete against each other. These appear as novelty classes such as 'Dog with the Longest Tail', 'Dog the Judge would like to take Home', 'Dog in Best Condition', 'Dog with the Most Appealing Eyes' and so on. For such shows the Kennel Club does not specify any special entry free or prize money, neither does it ask for a report on the results and awards. Prize cards throughout are white with black printing, unlike the usual show prize cards which are red for first, blue for second and yellow for third. Exemption shows must not be run in conjunction with any registered Canine Society or Training Club. However, the officers of such associations may organise or help to run them. Sometimes obedience tests of a simple nature can be incorporated too. These do not have to be similar to Kennel Club Obedience Tests. Exemption shows are usually held in aid of a charity, or at a public park show, often on a Bank Holiday.

LIMITED SHOWS

These are shows held under Kennel Club Rules and Regulations, so-called because entry is limited to a certain number of classes and restricted to members of clubs and societies, or to exhibitors within a specified radius or otherwise. Challenge Certificate winners are ineligible at Limited Shows. This type of show is unbenched.

SANCTION SHOWS

This type of show is also unbenched. It is confined to members of the club or society which is running the show and no Challenge Certificate winners are eligible. No class higher than Post-Graduate may be classified and only twenty classes are permitted when there is more than one breed or variety. When only one breed, such as the Cairn Terrier is concerned, the show must not comprise more than ten classes.

OPEN SHOWS

Such shows can be benched or otherwise. Very often they are held in conjunction with an Agricultural Show. No restrictions are made as to exhibitors making entries in the classes provided; conditions being similar to those at a Championship Show, but without the provision of Challenge Certificates.

CHAMPIONSHIP SHOWS

These are the most important shows and are really benched Open Shows held under the rules and regulations of the Kennel Club at which Challenge Certificates are offered and may be competed for. Some of the all-breed shows can occupy one, two or even three days, although Cruft's Dog Show, 1987 made the record with a great four-day show, indicative of the tremendous enthusiasm existing for dogs and dog shows in that year, and very likely to develop further. The specialist shows i.e. shows at which one breed such as Cairn Terriers might appear, are one-day events. Wins at these major shows qualify entrants for Cruft's which is the most important dog show in the world, catering for almost every variety, offering Challenge Certificates for most of them.

The late Walter Bradshaw ('Redletter') judging Mrs L. Z. Spence's Harlight Honeybunch at Northern Sporting Terrier show. Handler: Nicola Spence.

MATCHES

These are not dog shows in the strict sense of the words, but must not escape notice or mention for they are popular among doggy people and have been since the last century when pubs and hole-in-the-wall and corner venues used to enjoy the competitive atmosphere offered. These days they are conducted under Kennel Club rules and regulations and are based on the familiar knock-out system between pairs of dogs, a prize of some description being awarded to the final winner, *viz* Best Dog in Match. Clubs usually run these shows for member-education, either between dogs owned by club members or in challenge with dogs owned by members of rival clubs, either with the same breed or a different one.

Show preparation

TRAINING FOR SHOW

The first thing a show dog must learn is to be handled. This entails standing still while the judge goes over him from nose to tail, feeling, prodding, pushing and shifting all the time. This is where the judge will learn the extent of the dog's development, his structure and soundness.

He must get used to having his lips lifted for examination of his teeth; his private parts handled to ensure that he is entire and his forefeet lifted to examine his pads. A lot of dogs object to such things and those who do seldom get far in the show awards, for the judge quite rightly concurs that a dog who cannot be handled and assessed cannot be judged.

It is advisable, therefore, that when a promising puppy is about to try his luck in the show ring he should make his début fully trained in this performance and know how to accept such indignities with good grace. An ideal plan is to go through the typical actions of a judge with the dog at every given opportunity. Ask your friends to do the same when they visit you. Strangers too can be invited to run their hands over him, so that he gets used to the importunate handling routine and does not flinch from it. A lucky owner is he who owns a good puppy which proves to be a natural showman. This is a dog which does not seem to care how roughly he is pummelled by a judge and enjoys every minute of the show, acts in an orderly fashion, and even seems to demand attention when being exhibited. Given a dog like this – a sort of canine extrovert – there is no need to worry, for half the battle is won. However, most dogs can, with patience, be trained to perform well. It is clear that a good show prospect is worth a few hours training every week.

The best time to start a puppy on his show training course is just before his meal. The ideal place to do it is somewhere nice and quiet, away from all distractions, in a spare room or in the garden at home. If he has had already some of the elementary training discussed, he will have learned the pleasures of doing what he is told. In this, he will have to offer a good, fertile groundwork for this new type of instruction. He should be on his lead at all times during this course, just in the same way as you would have him 'dressed' in the show ring. Try him standing to see if he has a natural stance, i.e. a good firm standing position achieved without manual assistance. Occasionally, a dog has this natural attribute which usually comes from having an equable temperament, a well balanced physique and being structurally sound throughout. Made this way he will be able to 'show himself' independently of his handler. However, if it is seen that he does need some assistance in posing well then make sure that the way you place him is correct and that it displays his good points to advantage while minimising any faults he may possess.

Care should be taken not to spread him too wide in front. The Cairn's forelegs should be straight and parallel with each other from his laid-back shoulders down to the ground, the feet turned out slightly at the pasterns. Check on the forelegs in profile; they should run vertically from his withers to ground. If you put your palm between his legs and under his chest, then lift him slightly off the ground you should ease him down again to ground level briskly so that he falls into place naturally. By doing this a good exhibition position should be obtained. The front feet should be parallel with the feet of the rear limbs and a good guide to the right position will be to visualise the four feet in the four corners of an imaginary rectangle when viewed from above. Angulation of the hind limbs has to be considered too, so make sure that the hind feet have not fallen into a position too far forward or too much under the dog. Conversely, the hind limbs should not stretch out too far to the rear or will look as though the dog is sliding forward into a collapse!

A study should be made of successful show winners in the breed, whose published photographs usually indicate good positioning. Examine the various features depicted and these should be assessed, then emulated. As soon as the required position has been found and the dog placed in it, the command 'Stand!' should be given. Every time the dog is put down into place the command should be repeated. No doubt he will fidget at first, but with encouragement and the usual tit-bit reward for cooperative behaviour he will soon learn to 'stay-put' and eventually stand firm in his position even when handled by the judge. A danger exists with manual placing of this description that the exhibit will appear 'wooden'. He need not if his attention is maintained and enlivened with the anticipation of receiving a tit-bit which his owner should keep concealed in his hand. In any case, when he is in the ring he will find plenty of interesting dogs and activities to attract him, and, more important, to keep him on his toes. A puppy being trained this way should not have more than a ten minute lesson at a time. Youngsters get bored quickly and soon go stale with continued repetition. This must be avoided or progress will be retarded.

The time is now ripe for the puppy to show how well he can stand with distractions all round him. Up to now he has done very well in some quiet nook, but he will find the show ring a very noisy and busy place with more dogs together than he has ever seen before – quite apart from the throngs of people! A good idea for conditioning him to such a situation is to join the local dog-training club. Most of these bodies have their meetings in nearby halls or open air during clement weather and they cost little to join. Here, the puppy can be taken and get not only the dog-show atmosphere he needs to prepare him for his first proper show, but expert advice in the matters of deportment and posture, both important factors for him to learn in his forthcoming showring career. Here too, you will be able to deploy him around a ring or up and down so that he gets used to moving a typical distance up to and away from a presiding judge when the time comes for a real dog show. An effective way to get him to turn well in this promenade is to give a sharp snap of

Diana Hamilton judging Mrs L. Z. Spence's first Cairn at Bridlington in 1976. Handler: Nicola Spence.

the fingers when you drag on his lead to effect a smart turn about face. Do this consistently in conjunction with a guiding lead drag until you find he will do the turn automatically when he hears the snap, no lead pressures being needed. It makes your handling look slick and might well gain your exhibit an extra mark in the matter of ring deportment!

The pupil must be taught to move at a speed which suits him. At this correct speed he will show his good points to advantage while minimising the effect of his faults. A dog moved too fast or too slow will almost certainly achieve an unfavourable aspect in the ring. The true Cairn gait is distinct, treading neither wide nor narrow with the front feet, the hindquarter limbs showing some degree of parallelism when going away with ample spring, stride and rhythm. The action in all limbs has to be positive, neither weaving, ambling, fleeting, 'paddling' nor high-stepping. Such styles of action are perhaps desirable in some other breeds, but not in the Cairn. In this breed, well laid back shoulders, and nicely let down hocks are standard equipment and any specimen which is loose in shoulders, out-at-elbows or with upright shoulders and high hocks cannot possibly move correctly.

To produce good movement in the breed, it is necessary to fix both the structural details and pre-disposing nervous qualities genetically when breeding. When exhibiting, good selection and discrimination by a breeder should be evident in the exhibit's gait. It stands to reason that a dog when pulling or scrambling along on his lead will have his head thrust forward, his shoulders thrown out sideways and his forward action virtually impossible to assess. Alternatively, if he moves sluggishly, the beautiful and rhythmic muscular coordination we expect from the hindquarters of a moving Cairn is lost.

Teach the dog to make the best of himself at all times; it is just as important too that you yourself enter the ring with confidence. Then he will conduct himself in a well-behaved and hopefully professional manner. If you relax for just one moment, this might just be the fateful second when the judge turns on his heel to consider you for a prime placing. If your exhibit looks jaded and is sitting on his haunches instead of looking alert and up on his toes, then he does not deserve the prize he might have got. Ringcraft is an exhibitor's science. It needs to be studied with care and applied with skill. Others might have dogs as good as, even better than yours, but with your extra knowledge of the way to make the best of your Cairn, even to disguise his faults by clever and cautious display, your chances of beating them are enhanced.

Many judges like to judge small exhibits, such as Cairns, placed on a table. Your dog should be trained to get used to this procedure, hold his stance and show no objection or fear to being uplifted and examined so closely to the judge. However, to an inquiring judge a dog on the table is easier to assess than one on the showring floor. One can see better into a small dog's mouth and everyone knows that an exhibit with such a profuse coat as sported by the true Cairn can conceal a multitude of faults. An adjudicator well-versed in canine anatomy has full play with his hands over the dog from end to end – much easier than trying to discover faulty structural details, shoulders, stifles, hocks and ribs from floor level. Facial and skull features – eye colour, ear emplacement and expression – all are seen better and assessment thereby made easier all round.

Judging

Now that you have given your dog a good course of pre-show training, the time has come for the real thing. It will be realised that judging is really a matter of comparison – one dog against the other, point for point according to the Standard. This means taking one feature of the first dog against a similar feature possessed by a second exhibit, thus head for head, ears for ears and so on. At one time, a breed Standard had its own Scale of Points. Against this scale a judge would examine each dog and express points awarded for each feature, he would then tot these up and go on to the next dog, doing the same until he had got through the class of perhaps some ten or twenty. Such an arbitrary system did not work for it did not take into consideration those all-important characteristics – proportion, balance, breed type, and soundness. It therefore behoves a judge to have a clear understanding of the Standard before he enters the ring to offer his opinions on exhibitors' dogs. The breed is rich in good specialist judges, which is fortunate, for nothing debilitates a breed like Cairns than incompetent judging, whether it be inefficient or deliberate. Bad judging sets the fancy back a notch or two every time it happens. Ill-used exhibitors become rancorous, some even back out of the game, so dispirited do they feel. It is not only a disservice to a breed when incompetent judging occurs, but it very often closes the door to new, would-be fanciers.

A judge's ability is based on experience, the ownership of at least one good one – a champion perhaps, or maybe some consistent winners. The breed Standard is the 'bible' which tells us what the perfect Cairn Terrier should look like. Be assured, no one has seen a perfect Cairn yet, many are excellent but perfection has not turned up yet in spite of the fact that some owners think they have one at home. The judge must have a clear understanding of the Standard, an attribute which he would have built up in his mind by having absorbed the best points and features from every good dog he has seen which he has mentally fashioned into the best Cairn Terrier imaginable. His judging should be on the good points of the subject and not on its respective lack of faults for that is judging in a negative manner. He must look for type, soundness, pleasing balance with substance and ample bone. He must know how a Cairn should move and insist on conformity in action. Exaggeration should be deplored, especially in a bitch and showmanship should not be mistaken for quality. Breed type is of vital importance. It is difficult to describe, but broadly speaking breed type may be said to refer mainly upon the dog's anatomical structure and general appearance as against individual type which is seen more by points and detail.

It must be admitted that many judges have their fads or preferences in what makes a good Cairn Terrier. Such likes and dislikes are all right, but they must not exceed reasonable margins of commonsense. It has been noted that one judge will prefer one type of Cairn, whereas another pundit praises and supports another and different type. This set-up in the judging field is fallible, as there can be but one type – the right type – and every breeder should know it and strive for it in his own breeding target.

The show dog

The dog for exhibition must be prepared correctly for his début. He should have been brought into first class condition physically and mentally. His coat and general grooming must be superb and this would have been brought about by finest feeding and exercise, and his presentation be according to accepted Cairn Terrier fashion. Fortunately, there is not much involved in coat and outline preparation – just keep the tail and back of the forelegs free from too much back-under feathering and all is well. His movement has to be impeccable – a dog who moves badly will never reach the top in competition with those who excel in ring deportment. On a lead few dogs show themselves naturally, and the handler must be aware of his dog all the time he is in the ring, ensuring he is alert and standing properly and not being distracted by ringsiders, some known to him. You should keep an eye on everything which is going on around you, so that you can guide your exhibit into the positions which are most favourable to his best points and general appearance. Dog handling in the show ring still leaves a lot to be desired in the rank and file of exhibitors. You will find, therefore that if you can develop a smart and effective form of handling you will score points over slapdash and casual exhibitors. A little flamboyance will not come amiss providing it is kept within limits! Try and achieve all your work with the dog on a slack lead – it comes over much more effectively. Try not to make too much of a ritual out of your handling: some people 'top and tail' their exhibit, holding up its tail with the left hand and its head with the right. This type of craftsmanship often indicates a slack exhibit which cannot do either thing for itself, thus lacking the sort of eager, outgoing personality one expects to find in a good Cairn Terrier. In effect, it smacks of over-handling and could well irritate a judge. If your dog happens to be thrusting, and this is no crime in a Cairn, at least make sure that he does not upset the others in the ring.

Certain etiquettes prevail in dog showing and the exhibitor who ignores them soon becomes unpopular – never a good situation in such a highly competitive field. It seems hardly necessary to remark that a bitch in season should never be brought near to a show ring; her presence being enough to put every dog within sniffing distance right off his mark. Should you encounter another exhibitor acting selfishly and thoughtlessly in this respect, a word to the ring steward or show manager might prove useful and provide an official warning to the offender, encouraging him to remove his bitch. Remember that when you exhibit your dog you do so because you want to win – why else would you be

Remove dead and overlong hairs from shoulders and flanks

Shape tail to point. Broad at set~on

Remove any 'hanging' feather

Tail at set-on thick and well~furnished

Shape~up haunches

Clean~up inside hams

Shape around feet~ especially at back

Make clean around stifle area

Remove dead or untidy hair along back making level topline

Remove unwanted hair from behind ears

Produce a tidy underline and clean belly

Make tidy backs of legs

Remove superfluous hairs from TOP of ears. The rest should merge into head.

Lift out straggly dead hair in region of eyes

Cheeks~ Remove dead hair

Light trim below jaw

Remove dead and overlong hair from neck ruff

Clean up untidy frontal areas but leave hair adornment between legs

Remove untidy elbow hairs

The Cairn Terrier should be groomed daily and tidied-up generally. The main implements to use are your forefingers and thumb and a good plucking-grooming comb. Never use any professional cutting trimming tools, although you may have to employ scissors in a light manner when it comes to the feet. Most of your work will entail the removal of dead hair and untidy growth. Sharp manual plucking followed by close combing and brisk brushwork will achieve good results and the groom will soon learn to camouflage effectively his charge's little faults, remembering that a good judge may well discover them! If the toe-nails are too long these will require filing down, but this should be unnecessary if the dog had had adequate exercise on hard ground. An ideal length of coat to aim for is 2″ (5 cm) bearing in mind that it is better to take off too little rather than too much.

there in competition? It is not helpful to a dog if he keeps on losing, ringsiders and judges might well become thinking of him as an 'also-ran' and that is a bad cap to put on any show dog.

Show venue routine

Most shows are unbenched. Championship shows are benched and so are many Open shows. This means that when you visit the benched events you must carry a bench chain, obtainable from any pet store and of a length which can permit the dog to lie down comfortably yet restrictive enough to stop him interfering with or being interfered with by passing dogs en route for nearby positions in the venue. A blanket or similar which can be laid on the bench will offer him some comfort and it is always advisable to have such accoutrements cleaned when you return home. You should carry a water dish, first-aid kit and sandwiches also a flask of hot beverage for yourself. Most benched shows are at least one-day events, Cruft's goes on longer, often necessitating an overnight stay for out-of-town exhibitors. Make sure you have the dog's tit-bits well ensconced in your pocket or you may find your charge rebellious if these fail to appear in the ring. Have some food ready for him *after* he has been shown – do not feed him earlier at the show or you may make him sleepy and sluggish and unwilling to give of his best when shown. Check that your ring number (which you will have obtained from the show secretary in advance) corresponds with the number displayed on your bench. Put your personal belongings out of sight – putting them behind the dog itself is often the best place, although not necessarily if you have a Cairn who loves everybody!

If your show is unbenched, and most of them are, the routine will be less stringent and formal. Then, you can place yourself and your dog anywhere in the room or field of action. Comfortably situated, stop there until it is time for you to enter the class. Once in, the ring steward will direct you into a position with other entrants. The judge will put himself either at one end of the ring or in the centre. He will start with one end of the line and call over to him the first entrant. Should this be you, then walk the dog across to him; he will probably want you to place your exhibit on a table so that he can examine it closely. Most judges prefer to do this with small breeds, for you can see much more of the dog at table top level than bending down to the ground. A wise judge will have been watching you approach him, assessing the dog's action and general appearance, i.e. getting an impression of the exhibit. He will probably ask you the animal's age. You should do no more than answer the questions he puts to you. He does not want to know what the dog had for breakfast, that it was sick on the way up or that it won a first prize or was robbed of deserved awards only the week previously. If you persist in unwanted conversation he might feel inclined to deduct points which the dog hasn't deserved to lose. He will then ask you to turn the dog around as he goes over its body and contours, examining its head, mouth, eye colour, ears for size and emplacement, coat texture, front, depth of chest, ribs, bone, front and rear limbs, feet and pads. He will assess balance, set-on of tail, and genitals in the case of a male. Satisfied with these tests, he will ask you to replace the dog on the ground and move it away from him; then he will see the quality of its hind action, tail carriage and rear-end balance. You will parade the length of the ring, turn around and come back, approaching the judge so that he can assess the dog's forward action, observing whether he 'paddles' his feet as he moves and whether the dog holds up his head without having it dragged up by lead pressure. At the close of this stage the judge has usually finished with you and directs you back to your position in the line. Sometimes a judge likes to have you walk round him so that he can assess side action and balance and to catch sight of the dog's shoulder formation as he circles the ring. However, most judges seek imperfections manually when the exhibit is up on the table. All the time you are engaged with this 'performance' you must keep on your toes and never slacken your attention on the judge or on your dog at the end of the lead.

The judge will be expected to place his winners as follows: 1st (red card), 2nd (blue card), 3rd (yellow card) and Reserve (green card). Sometimes VHC (Very Highly Commended) and HC (High Commended) cards are awarded for fifth and sixth places. These are merely commendation cards and never carry official prize money, although sometimes a club will apply a token award for the winners. If you win anything, take it with a smile and a thank you, even if you thought your dog should have done better. It is essential that as you progress in the show world your name is coupled with that of sportsmanship.

Show conclusions

Sportsmanship and jealousy both show up prominently in dog show life. All competition work brings out jealousy in its ranks – it is inevitable. People try to be good sportsmen but often seem to fail when their dogs get beaten! If there arises any suspicion that their losing was occasioned by unfair judication then they seethe with rage and very often lose interest in dogs and dog-showing. This is a pity, for had they persisted exhibiting the very near future might well have seen them winning top prizes. It should be remembered that if every judge judged and thought the same, there would be little use in having dog shows; the same dog winning every time and the rest with no hope of entering the cards.

You have to see the game in the light it was intended when dog showing commenced a century ago. Sometimes you win, the next week you lose; judges vary in their thoughts about any breed. Some may prefer one type, others lean towards a different type; the average exhibitor soon gets to know his judges and their foibles and fads. A certain amount of leeway in their opinions can be tolerated, but it should be remembered that there is only one type, that being the correct type and that is what should be judged too. Whether a judge approves of all the points demanded in the breed Standard is his own affair but when he judges he should enter the ring with a clear mental picture of a perfect Cairn based on the Standard of the breed and confine his judging to that model example.

When exporting

The Cairn Terrier fancy has a highly commendable code of ethics, as we have already shown. This code must apply particularly to dealings with overseas buyers who have put their faith in obtaining a good sound dog and a square deal from any selected U.K. kennel.

It is vitally important that only first-class stock should be sent abroad. If it is to be exhibited, then great care must be taken to send stock of the

Uniquecottage Bronze Wing, best in show CTA Open Show, 1986 with judge Mrs S. Roskell. Owner: Mrs Parker Tucker. (*Gibbs*)

Ch. Sugar Plum of
Courtrai, owned by the
Misses Howes & Clark.
(*Anne Roslin-Williams*)

correct type of a sort which will appeal to local judges. The problem in
determining such a matter is not so critical in Western European
countries where there is a constant interchange of competent judges
whose interpretation of the Cairn breed Standard varies little. This
situation applies to America as well, but in some localities, it has been
noted that local champions, often big winners, do not look too much like
the Cairns whose type we seek to achieve in Great Britain. In fact, some
Cairns seen are often indistinguishable from West Highland Whites,
except in the matter of colour. The salient point is that these specimens,
smart, personable and sound, teeming with type (of a sort), have
established themselves as typical Cairns in their homeland. Consequently, when you, as an exporter send out a Cairn of excellent type
from this country, you may find it losing sadly to local champions merely
on the basis of an established, possibly wrong type. You can imagine the
disappointment experienced by the new owner.

It is incumbent upon an exporter to send abroad specimens which
come as near as possible to correct type, as we in the breed's U.K.
homeland, understand it. The dog should have no defect in gait,
temperament or faulty dentition – in fact, there should be nothing which

Ch. Harlight Heidi, owned by Mrs L. Z. Spence. (*Anne Roslin-Williams*)

a local judge can seize upon to excuse or justify a deliberate or otherwise unfavourable placing. This applies particularly to a breed in which little or no trimming is practised. With a well coated variety a clever exhibitor will contrive to conceal often quite serious faults in his dog, but in the non-trim breeds such as the Cairn, every blemish in physical make up is much easier to discover.

While concluding on the matter of exporting, some breeders who have the opportunity of sending their stock abroad at favourable prices and with the chance to establish their kennel names abroad in the right places, hesitate to do so for fear that the exercise will prove difficult and tedious and fraught with incident. These fears need not deter. There are a number of totally reliable dog exporting firms to be used, all you have to do is to consult them, give them the facts and they will quote you for sending your Cairn from A to B, safely and surely and covered with an adequate insurance. They will do all the ground work and ensure that the dog arrives at his destination, is met and transported to his new home. Of course, you must see all the documentation through in a proper professional manner, but that constitutes no problem – The Kennel Club is there to guide and help you.

7 The Cairn in Sickness and Disease

Although your veterinary surgeon is the right and proper person to consult when your dog is sick or hurt it is useful to be able to recognise the symptoms of virus and bacterial disease as well as the more common ailments by which the average dog is often beset. In the following section, which is necessarily brief, first aid measures are given and these should be determined and administered with care pending arrival of the expert.

Immunisation

Having your dog immunised against the dreaded diseases of Distemper, Hard Pad, Hepatitis and Leptospirosis today constitutes no problem. Every veterinary surgeon is able to fulfil this service for a nominal fee. The various vaccines which have been developed by veterinary science are available according to one's personal preference and one's country. It is advisable to discuss the matter of immunisation with your own veterinary surgeon and be guided by him. No matter whether your Cairn is valuable or not he has a right to the protection these vaccines can offer. The age at which a puppy should be inoculated will vary according to the proprietary brand of the vaccine. Some require a youngster to be about two months old for the 'shot' to be effective whereas others prefer the puppy to be at least twelve weeks of age. With all vaccines it is wise to check whether 'booster' shots are recommended; these being given every one or two years thereby establishing maximum lasting protection. The fact that your dog has been adequately covered against the incidence of disease should not prevent you from exercising every normal precaution for at least ten days following the inoculation. This will allow the antibodies reasonable time to rally against any attack by canine virus or bacteria. The natural antibiotic defence in the Cairn Terrier whelp is given by a substance called Colostrum, referred to in the chapter on Whelping. This exists in a dam's initial flow of milk for at least twenty-four hours. It is a globulinous matter which acts as a natural immuniser against disease for the first few weeks of the puppy's life, its effects tapering away almost up to the later point when man-made vaccines have to be injected for continuity of protection. This is why hand-reared youngsters, i.e. puppies who have never savoured their dam's true milk, are usually more prone to disease than others unless their deficiency is corrected by artificial means.

Immunity of about three weeks can be given against the virus diseases of Distemper, Hard Pad and Hepatitis, using appropriate vaccines approved by your veterinary surgeon. The dog owner is well advised to study his Cairn closely, understand his nature, characteristics and pattern of his habits, so that anything unusual in his manner will serve as a warning light to the watcher, preparing him for further signs of sickness. Make sure you know that a dog's normal temperature should be 101.4°F – although small puppies sometimes register half a degree more than this. Any temperature over 102.5°F is one for concern, but if it is 103°F and over, then the dog should be isolated immediately and the veterinary surgeon called in. Sub-normal temperatures of say, 100°F require close attendance of the patient pending veterinary diagnosis, this excluding the normal temperature of 99°F or less, of an in-whelp bitch about to have her puppies. Keep by you a good quality half-minute blunt-end clinical thermometer. To use this correctly first shake down the mercury in the stem below 97°F. Lightly smear the bulb end with 'Vaseline', then gently insert for one minute into the dog's anus, holding him steady meanwhile so that he does not jerk away, or try to sit down, thereby smashing the instrument. The temperature can be read and the thermometer thoroughly disinfected after use. Make sure that you hold a good stock of bandages in various widths, also that reliable antiseptic and disinfectant preparations are at hand. Avoid those which have a high and permeating aroma – dogs do not like such scents overmuch. The wise dog owner will know too just where he can lay his hands on suitable size splints in case of a broken limb. Cotton wool should be easily available, also the common poison antidotes like salt, mustard, washing soda and hydrogen peroxide, items to be found in most households. Information as to how these should be used to make a poisoned dog vomit is well worth acquiring as immediate action can well save a dog's life.

Major ailments

CANINE PARVOVIRUS ENTERITIS
This tiny virus (its diameter is less than one-millioneth of an inch) is one which causes some apprehension in the dog breeder. It is a comparatively new disease, being unknown prior to 1978. Similar to feline

enteritis its symptoms are severe and the gastro-enteritis experienced is such that death often occurs. It usually affects the puppy just out of weaning stage, although sometimes the older dog is affected. The virus is unusual in that it reaches the intestine by way of the circulatory system instead of passing through the alimentary tract. It would appear that an infected dog could pass on the disease either by contact or by its excretions. Temperature can be either normal or sub-normal and faeces are frequently blood-stained. Heart failure is often caused by damage to the heart muscle.

Immediate veterinary attention is called for when the disease is suspected. Incubation period is fifty-four days, infected animals vomiting followed by diarrhoea. Veterinary treatment will include fluid therapy and antibiotics. There is an excellent live vaccine available now in the veterinary world and this will invoke a high level of protection. It is given initially at fifteen weeks, although some vets recommend it be given first at six weeks and again at fifteen weeks. It is important to maintain booster doses annually. Breeders are still watching anxiously the progress of this vaccine which is being well publicised.

COCCIDIOSIS

This is very infectious and an entire kennel can be quickly affected. The parasite is not unlike the one which attacks fowl; it lives in the small intestines and causes severe diarrhoea often marked with blood. The dog loses weight very quickly, and seems to lose all interest in life. It is important to harden up the motions and the first move in achieving this is to take the dog off all meat, confining him to milky meals. As the disease is spread via the faeces it is essential to maintain absolute cleanliness throughout the kennel, swabbing down with warm water and disinfectant several times a day. The veterinary surgeon will be able to ease the position and hasten the cure.

DISTEMPER

At one time this virus disease was a scourge on dogdom. It usually attacks a puppy within his first year but any age of dog can contract the disease which is very infectious and is capable of wiping out an entire kennel. Although a victim of the disease can recover, there exists an unpleasant aftermath which is liable to affect the dog's nervous system, possibly his brain. This after-effect is known as Chorea, which is like St Vitus' Dance, and parts of the body and limbs twitch convulsively and there appears no cure or even much relief.

However, the disease is only of moderate consequence today, as it is

Toptwig Brown Sugar of Gayclan, owned by Mr E. Loader (1975). (*Anne Roslin-Williams*)

easily controlled by the many excellent vaccines now produced by veterinary chemists. Distemper causes inner body inflammation, the initial symptoms being loss of appetite, lassitude, some sickness and discharge from the eyes and nostrils. The eyes will become bloodshot and 'gummed up' and should be carefully swabbed over with a mild solution of boric acid or similar. Food will later be rejected completely and the dog will stand in a tucked-up position suggestive of abdominal pain. There will be a dry, hoarse cough and an antipathy to strong light. Odorous, dark-coloured diarrhoea can be expected, also vomiting, the temperature being around 103°F.

The patient should be nursed quietly in a darkened room, cleaning him up at regular intervals and with minimum fuss. Light feeding such as boiled water into which a little honey has been stirred is ideal and should be continued, gradually increasing to easily digested rather more solid foods as the patient mends. Ensure that the dog's living quarters (which of course must be completely isolated from the main kennel) are airy yet warm and draught-free.

The best way to prevent the occurrence of this unpleasant disease is to have a puppy inoculated when he is about three months of age. There are a number of different methods of immunisation, all good, as far as is known. 'Booster' doses should follow later in life to maintain immunity, but your veterinary surgeon will advise you on all these matters.

HARD PAD

This is actually a more virulent 'cousin' of Distemper, the symptoms being similar although even less pleasant than that disease. Strictly speaking, it is a form of Encephalitis and therefore serious. Following on to the usual symptoms of Distemper there is a stage when the pads of the feet swell and harden, hence the name given to the disease. Possibly the swelling will be noted on the dog's facial points and soft parts around the abdomen. The patient will lapse into a fever and may froth at the mouth, finally reaching a stage of spasms and convulsions which usually end fatally.

Treatment is as for Distemper, but a successful vaccine has been developed and used in conjunction with the one for Distemper and Hepatitis, the inoculation being given usually in one shot. In America the disease is named paradistemper.

HEPATITIS

Correctly known as Canine Virus Hepatitis, also Rhubarth's Disease, this can speedily prove fatal unless dealt with immediately, young stock succumbing easily to the virus. The disease inflames and damages the liver and blood vessels, especially in a bitch. The symptoms are again somewhat similar to those of Distemper, notably loss of appetite with acute thirst, severe gastro-enteritis with vomiting and diarrhoea, a high temperature up to 106°F and prostration. It is an insidious disease and a dog might give every sign of having recovered from it, only to collapse and expire a few hours later. A marked jaundice is usually indicative of oncoming convulsions to warn an owner of this sad end. It is believed that the virus remains active in some victims months after reported recovery. It can have the effect of inducing sterility, again especially in a bitch.

A reliable vaccine is available used in conjunction with preventative immunisation against Distemper and Hard Pad.

LEPTOSPIROSIS (*Spirochaete*)

Two forms of leptospiral disease are known to veterinary science. Leptospira jaundice (*L. ichterohaemorrhagica*) known as Weils Disease comes from contact with brown rat urine. It attacks the dog's liver, causing jaundice and haemorrhage, frequently proving fatal. The dog goes off its food and lies around in a tucked-up position. Jaundice is noted in the membranes of eyes and mouth. It is a serious condition and requires early treatment with anti-serum and antibiotics. Obviously, it is necessary to destroy all the rats around the place and other canine inmates should be injected with vaccine as a preventative measure. Subsequent booster doses must not be overlooked. The other form, Canicola Fever (*L. canicola*) which passes from an infected dog to other victims, is somewhat lesser in its effect, although the bacteria is believed to damage the kidneys. Dogs affected can be seemingly cured, the vaccines available being very reliable, also large doses of penicillin have been used to good effect. The possibility of kidney disease damage can be offset at least to some extent with high grade protein feeding such as fresh raw meat, cheese, eggs, etc. The symptoms of an infected dog are similar to those found in Distemper, together with a high fever which entails the patient's complete isolation from his fellows, treatment being given as advised by the veterinary surgeon. Loss of weight, diarrhoea, intense depression, a strong desire to sleep and some jaundice (yellowing) in the whites of the eyes will be noted. The temperature usually registers around 104°F. It is not a lengthy sickness and the phase has often passed after a week. Note that this disease is sometimes known as Stuttgart Disease when it is in an advanced form showing pungent smelling ulcers around the mouth, a stage which often proves fatal.

PROGRESSIVE RETINAL ATROPHY (P.R.A.)
This is a congenital disease of the eye and one which is mentioned here as causing much trouble in *general* canine circles, but Cairns seem free from it, fortunately. It is hereditary and broadly speaking one would say that any animal which suffers from it must have received the genes for such blindness from both parents, although neither parent may be actually blind. Thus, the genes for such blindness are recessive. If the gene for blindness is carried by one parent only, then the offspring will not be blind, but will be carries for blindness. If however, both parents carry one gene each for blindness (though not blind themselves) they themselves are carriers. If both genes come together their offspring may be blind or they may inherit one gene each and be carriers. But the difficulty is to know which puppies may be carriers and which may be sound. If any question of blindness occurs it is extremely unwise to continue breeding the sire and dam, although the fault probably lies latent in the grandparents on either the paternal or maternal side. The symptoms rarely manifest themselves until a dog is mature, so unless one is suitably forewarned it is extremely difficult to weed out the culprits until too late. There is an excellent BVA/KC Scheme in operation for certain breeds and much work has been done on the problem by Mr G. C. Knight, FRCVS, DVR, the well-known veterinarian.

RABIES
Although virtually unknown in Britain, the 1969 scare which meant the extermination of many wild animals in and around a Surrey town made people aware of its implications. The disease is an ancient one, still very common in India and the East, affecting the dog's functional nervous

system when the virus is introduced into his blood stream. The bite of a rabid dog is therefore likely to cause rabies or hydrophobia (fear of water) as it is sometimes known. The victim is unable to drink because of paralysis in the throat and frothing at the mouth is also a symptom. An acute change in the dog's normal behaviour pattern can be expected, and he will usually become snappy, even vicious. This propensity increases with dropping of the lower jaw and progressive paralysis of the hind limbs especially. The dog will wander away from home and this is when the real danger starts for he may bite and infect other animals, wild and domestic, who in turn can bite others who then become secret carriers of the virus. Humans are equally prone to the disease which eventually works its way to the brain, resulting in death. Several countries, notably Great Britain, employ a system of animal quarantine to guard against rabies. This, although considered severe by some has proved its efficacy on innumerable occasions. There is no guaranteed cure announced, as yet, but useful veterinary vaccines are now available which will immunise your dog against this unpleasant and powerful virus.

TETANUS

This is usually known as lockjaw. It is not common in dogs, but it should be watched for and if encountered dealt with by an appropriate vaccine which is available. The germ strikes through an open wound, producing a poison capable of striking the nerves and causing severe muscular contraction. The patient will move stiffly and occasionally twitch when standing or even at rest. The best treatment is to nurse him in a darkened room, giving the dog light tasty meals. Ask the veterinary surgeon to prescribe a sedative as he will almost certainly be suffering from shock.

Minor ailments and physical conditions

ABNORMAL BIRTH

When a puppy arrives head first at the opening of the womb this is a normal birth. When the hind feet are presented first, it is known as a breech birth and although not normal, seldom offers any complications. Puppies presented sideways or in twisted form will probably need veterinary assistance, according to the seriousness of the situation.

ABNORMALITIES

These usually entail congenital deformities, *viz* Cleft Palate, Hare Lip – the two conditions often appearing together. The normally flat roof of the mouth is cleft, making it impossible for the puppy to suckle its dam as no vacuum can be formed in the mouth. The milk will bubble out

Summers of Pyeknowle, owned by Miss Dewhurst. (*Anne Roslin-Williams*)

through the whelp's nose and it will not thrive, dying within a day or so. It should be humanely destroyed at once.

ABORTION

A bitch will abort her puppies, usually due to a knock or blow, or even infection in the uterus. If abortion occurs early in the gestation period, the dam will sometimes dispose of them herself without the owner's knowledge. This is sometimes taken by the breeder as a 'miss' and a free stud service claimed! Symptoms when noted in a bitch in whelp are extreme fatigue, sickness and haemorrhage at the vulva.

ABSCESS

A hard painful swelling filled with pus, such as a boil. It can be caused by localised grime and is more likely to affect a dog temporarily out of condition. Raise the swelling to a head with fomentations, then squeeze away the poison matter. Dress carefully after swabbing the wound with a mild antiseptic.

ACCIDENT

In the case of internal damage and to offset shock condition, keep the dog quiet in a warm, dark room. Reassure him with words and caresses until arrival of the veterinary surgeon.

ACNE

This is seen in pus-filled pimples which eventually break forming scabs. The rash is usually found on the under-belly and is very irritating. Witch hazel dressing and medicinal powder will normally deal effectively with the condition, but it is prudent to get your veterinary surgeon's opinion.

ANAL GLANDS

There are two small glands beneath your Cairn's tail, one on either side of the anus. An inheritance from the wild state, they are no longer used by the domestic dog. They become clogged with waste matter, causing inflammation and irritation. The dog will rub his rear along the ground and appears in some distress. The trouble can be eased by squeezing the glands to expel the offending substance. This operation should be attended to regularly as there is always a danger that abscesses might form.

APPETITE

Lack of: In small puppies this is usually a sign of worms, which must be expelled allowing the youngster to revert to normal feeding. In older dogs it could indicate a soreness in the mouth, causing the dog pain when eating. Examine the teeth and gums and soft part of the underlip. Always take the dog's temperature in case he is sickening for something, as loss of appetite is an initial symptom of the virus diseases.

Perverted: It is not uncommon to find dogs, especially puppies and bitches, eating coke, coat, stones, even their own excrement and that of other dogs. Again, this may be due to worms, but the usual cause is some chemical deficiency in the bloodstream which can be corrected either by change of diet (with an emphasis on raw meat) or vitamin additives.

Abnormal: A bitch in whelp will usually increase her food intake. It is a common symptom just prior to her *oestrum*, in any case. The phase frequently reverts back to normal, but the owner should regulate meal quantities meanwhile.

ARTIFICIAL RESPIRATION

The whelping dam uses this system to induce breath into her new born puppies. She prods, pushes and tumbles them with her tongue until they 'squeal' into life. A puppy which fails to respond can be resurrected by giving it the 'kiss of life' and a dog almost drowned can be brought to life by laying it on its side and depressing the ribs with the flat palm of the hand. Release at once, and repeat the pressure alternately every two seconds.

ASTHMA

A complaint which usually affects older dogs, especially those carrying too much weight. Breathlessness and wheezing respiration are to be expected, sometimes accompanied by a dry cough. If allowed to persist the heart can be affected. However, a change of diet to include mainly fresh, raw meat is necessary, also the gradual stepping up of daily exercise in order to reduce the dog's weight. The veterinary surgeon should be informed so that he can prescribe professionally.

BALANITIS

A discharge from the penis, probably commoner in a dog not used at stud than one in regular service. A mild solution of antiseptic (dilution of 1:5 in tepid water) should be syringed beneath the sheath at regular intervals until the condition is relieved.

BITES

Providing the dog can reach the affected area and lick it clean, this will prove the speediest cure. However, if the bite is in an awkward and inaccessible place, wash the immediate region and treat with a good antiseptic solution. If the cuts are deep and open drip in iodine or antiseptic first, then bandage and prevent the dog from relieving himself of the dressing by using a conventional Elizabethan Collar which your veterinary surgeon will prescribe.

BLADDER

The best aid for reducing bladder inflammation is to flush out the system with plenty of water, but it is not easy to get a dog to drink more than he wishes at any one time. The usual cause of this condition is Cystitis and it is advisable therefore to get veterinary advice. If stones are the cause, then it may be necessary to employ surgery to remove them, although there are scientific systems which effect stone removal these days, which are expensive. Incontinence, i.e. inability to hold water in the bladder is usually found in bitches heavily in whelp or in old dogs. When an in-whelp bitch is so affected she may be worried by her lapses and need her owner's patience and understanding, for this is no more than a brief phase and she will quickly return to her usual standard of house-cleanliness. In an old dog it might well indicate kidney disorder in which case your veterinary surgeon should be asked to examine the dog and prescribe.

BLINDNESS

A puppy is born blind and seldom opens his eyes until the ninth or tenth day of his life. Congenital blindness on the other hand is a serious matter, progressive retinal atrophy (P.R.A.), i.e. night-blindness, being a worrying problem in the general dog world today. The condition is one for the expert and advice should be sought without delay. An animal so affected must not be considered fit for any breeding programme. *See also* Cataracts.

BREASTS
Congestion of breasts is often encountered when a bitch's milk is not taken up quickly enough by her whelps, causing encrustment around the teats. Inflammation occurs and the bitch becomes distressed, biting at herself and sometimes inducing abscesses. Her fluid intake should be reduced at once and the teats bathed around to reduce and dispose of the 'caking'. She should then be milked by hand and your veterinary surgeon should be asked to prescribe a remedy in order to ease her discomfort.

BREATH
Bad breath is not uncommon in dogs of advanced years. It is often caused by tartar lining the teeth and ulceration in the lip area. Constipation and sundry infections can also induce bad breath. All dental areas likely to be responsible should be swabbed with a mild solution of antiseptic and the dog's teeth scaled and cleaned.

BREATHING
Laboured breathing is usually found in an out-of-condition dog, especially after he has exercised. It may suggest anaemia or a heart condition in which case the veterinary surgeon should be asked to examine the patient.

Ch. Clanronald Tam O'Shanter, owned by Miss J. M. Hudson. (*Anne Roslin-Williams*)

BRONCHITIS

This is frequently contracted after a soaking or a bad cold. Dogs allowed to sleep in a draught will sometimes become bronchial, coughing and wheezing and with a high temperature of about 103.5°F. It is important to bed them down in a warm, airy atmosphere, giving light, tasty meals. In bad cases, the Bronchitis Kennel will have to be employed, the patient being forced to breathe in vapour of Friars' Balsam or similar medication.

BURNS

Always treat for shock as well as the localised damage. The dog should be kept quiet in a dark, warm room and be reassured by his owner. A teaspoonful of bicarbonate of soda and warm milk with glucose added should be administered. Burn ointment should be stored ready for such an emergency, but failing this, first-aid measures will include sponging with strong, newly made tea at blood heat. This applies only to mild burns and scalds. Higher degree cases should be referred at once to your veterinary surgeon. When convalescing the patient should be fed high protein, especially fresh, raw meat.

CANKER

Ear canker is not uncommon in Cairns, although it is more usual in drop-eared breeds such as Spaniels. It is a condition affecting the inner ear canal. There is inflammation and discharge of a brown substance which is waxy and smells unpleasantly. It needs careful cleaning away from the ear and this is best effected by using a small tight wad of cotton wool wrapped around the blunted end of an orange stick (cotton 'buds' can be obtained from any chemist) and the wax teased out, an operation which needs to be done very gently. The main symptoms of the condition are seen in the way the dog shakes his head, carries it uncomfortably to the side and scratches his ears. There are a number of medications such as drops and powders on the market to deal with canker and one or more of these can be employed successfully by the average dog owner. Sometimes due to the intense irritation canker will cause the dog, it may prove necessary to give him a mild sedative before he beds down for the night.

CATARACTS

The lenses of the eyes will become covered by a milky film in advanced cases, the sight then being seriously affected. The condition is often found in older dogs, but cataracts can be inherited and young Cairns with such a legacy from their ancestors can seldom be treated satisfactorily even with expert surgery; even then the dog will only be likely to see objects at a modest fixed distance.

CHOREA

In humans this is equivalent to 'St Vitus' Dance' and is the aftermath of Distemper. The symptoms are mainly confined to an uncontrollable shake with twitching which may extend over the body. It is incurable, although the condition can be eased with sedatives and medicinal salts which will be prescribed by your veterinary surgeon. Fortunately, as we see little of Distemper these days it follows that Chorea is rarely encountered.

CHOKING

This has to be treated as an emergency, for it is probably caused by some foreign object lodged in the dog's throat. To remove it, two people should be employed, one to prise open and hold steady the dog's jaws, the other to hook out with his index finger the offending object.

To offset the possibility of such accidents, take care to keep all lethal objects like tiny rubber balls, knobbly small bones and children's toys out of a dog's reach. Cut up his meat into safe chunks too; a greedy dog can easily choke on a piece of unmanageable size, although often enough he manages to vomit it up safely.

COLIC

Stomach pains brought on by the dog eating something which does not agree with him. The symptoms include a tucked-up position indicative of severe pain. The best medicine if colic is diagnosed is a small teaspoonful of bicarbonate of soda in warm milk. Following this, let the patient rest in a warm room.

COLITIS

Inflammation of the colon, diarrhoea and loss of weight being normal symptoms. As in humans it is not a very satisfactory condition to treat, but in the initial stages milky meals are best coupled with a diet of a nutritious nature with nursing in a warm room. This will have good effect and allow a useful interim period for the easement of lining inflammation. Charcoal powder, one teaspoonful a day over the evening meal will help considerably.

COLLAPSE

Only a serious malady is likely to cause complete collapse in a dog, although often it can be occasioned by shock, following a fight or an accident. Animals so affected may well have a weak heart, but in any case, always treat for shock, raising the dog's hindquarters above head level with the patient laid on his right side. If he is conscious two drops of brandy on the back of his tongue will help, otherwise give nothing orally. All cases of collapse require veterinary attention.

CONCUSSION

A heavy blow on the head will cause this and the dog should be at once put into a dark room and the veterinary surgeon called. Ice packs can be applied to the dog's head and he should be well bolstered around with stone hot water bottles covered with blankets for insulation.

CONJUNCTIVITIS

Inflammation of the eyelids around the inner edge, causing watering and soreness. It can be caused by injury and foreign bodies entering the eyes such as sand, dust or pollen. The condition is always likely to recurr, but can be treated with the application of a warm saline solution or ointment prescribed by your veterinary surgeon. It is important to ensure that the condition does not persist as, once deep-seated, ulceration may develop and in the chronic state there can exist some danger of blindness.

CONSTIPATION

This is usually due to too much biscuit type meal with insufficient vegetable oil matter. The dog's motions should be monitored carefully every day and wrong feeding will soon become apparent. It can be caused also by inadequate food intake or be due to illness, muscular weakness due to debility or lack of fresh air and exercise. The first approach to the problem must be with roughage in the form of wholemeal biscuit and cereal foods with a good balance of meat and vegetable juices in the meals. Cod liver oil or liquid paraffin in teaspoonful doses can be given, olive oil is possibly better in summer, but the course of application should be brief, say seven days at a time as such oils are liable to absorb Vitamin-D from the system. Purgatives may be used, but these must be of a gentle nature and infrequent – such medicines are best obtained from your veterinary surgeon or from a well recommended proprietary source.

If constipation persists in the dog, it is advisable to have a check made to ensure that no unnatural cause exists. A blockage in the bowel can cause severe pain, vomiting, the passing of blood and a dog is usually in dire straights, requiring immediate surgical intervention.

CRAMP

Although this usually occurs when a dog has spent lengthy periods in close quarters is given free rein of exercise, relief and correction can soon be achieved by simple massage treatment. The condition is not hereditary in the Cairn as in related forms.

CYSTITIS (*See* Bladder Inflammation)

CYSTS

The commonest form of cyst is interdigital, that which appears between the dog's toes. He will be in some pain and attempt to lick the swellings, either making them worse or bringing them to a pustular head so that they eventually burst. Failing this, each foot should be put in warm water or hot fomentations applied and a mild antiseptic solution swabbed over the wound once the pus has been dispersed. Final dressing should be with medicated powder. Cysts sometimes appear on the body and these should be sought during the Cairn's daily grooming as they are not readily seen beneath his profuse coat. However, before surgery is envisaged or local treatment given, it is advisable to experiment with the dog's diet. A complete change of feeding, i.e. from raw fresh meat to a good proprietary brand of dog food or vice versa has been known to dispose of cysts within two weeks. If the remedy lies in such a method it must be preferable to any other involving surgery.

DIABETES

The two main symptoms are thirst and hunger. The coat becomes dry and staring and general condition poor. Lassitude, vomiting and diarrhoea occur and the condition is normally a condition for the veterinary surgeon to treat. Home treatment could include a sprinkle of bicarbonate of soda over every meal which should be mainly of raw meat, once the motions have been made firmer. It is better to feed in the mornings only, withholding food and water in the latter part of the day.

It is probable that the veterinary surgeon will prescribe tranquillisers to keep night incontinence in check and suggest a dosage to encourage appetite. The situation may require careful, possibly extended nursing, but most patients return to full health.

DIARRHOEA

This is a symptom, often a precursor of many disorders as well as the virus diseases, already mentioned. It is the body's way of disposing its toxic substances which have upset the digestive system. Diarrhoea should be a warning to an owner to seek its cause, making sure whether it is merely a simple case of worms or part of the pattern of serious infection. If the condition continues for two days the veterinary surgeon must be called for consultation without further delay. Feeding should be confined to warm bread and milk which will help bind the motions and make them firm; no raw meat should be allowed until diagnosis has been made. Other dogs in the kennel should be kept away from the patient's motions in case of infection.

DISCHARGES

Any form of discharge is usually indicative of infection and it is wise to call in the veterinary surgeon to ascertain its cause. Mucous discharge from the nose suggests virus disease; ear discharge, a form of canker; and vaginal discharge, while being common enough in bitches soon after whelping, is a debilitating condition capable of developing into peritonitis if not halted. Any unusual discharge should be suspect and dealth with summarily. Penis discharge (Balanitis) has been dealt with already and discharges from the mouth suggest bad teeth or ulceration of the lips or folds of skin.

DISCHISIATIS

In effect, a double row of eyelashes turning in slightly from the lids and brushing the eyeballs, causing the dog great discomfort. Surgery would appear the best way of dealing with this matter, for extraction of the lashes with tweezers from time to time does little more than to relieve the situation.

DOMESTIC HAZARDS

The home and garden offer their own dangers to the family dog. Care should be taken to ensure that all garden tools and implements are put away when not in use. There are many sharp edges involved with some of these things which if left upturned and unattended can prove lethal to an enquiring and curious pet. Open shears and upturned rakes present particular hazards and live cables connected with electric garden machines often prove tempting to some creatures inclined to nibble at anything before them. Pest control chemicals and baits when eaten or brought into contact with a dog can kill or at least render the creature very sick. Some plants are poisonous too; and this danger exists mainly in spring when the tannin content of the sap is at its peak, although acorns fallen around the bases of oak trees can cause sickness, even severe upset in some animals. The foxglove (*Digitalis purpurea*) can cause severe stomach pains and the popular garden shrub, Rhododendron holds toxins in its leaves, flowers, nectar and pollen. The common

Buttercup (*Ranunculus acris*) and the commonly known St Anthony's Turnip (*R. bulbous*) are reputed to cause poisoning. The bark and pods, especially the latter in the case of Laburnum cause intense sickness if ingested in quantity. The large blade leaves of the Rhubarb (*Rheum rhaponticum*) contain an irritant poison capable of upsetting an animal. These are only a few of the many plants to be encountered in a private garden.* Most of the poisoning can be countered, if in good time, by inducing vomiting in the patient, but it is an odd fact that some animals after cure will often return to the very plant which upset them to eat some more!

In the home itself, the kitchen with its boiling fluids and hot foods presents danger and with so many detergents and caustic cleaning preparations around it is not surprising that some fatalities occur. Cigarette and cigar ends left lying about will often be chewed and eaten by puppies, frequently with dire results. Headache pills and other medicines, often left unattended must be kept out of the way of pets for obvious reasons. Rubber bands and plastic bags in which food has been stored are hazards to a dog in various ways. It must be remembered that if you are in doubt as to a wise course of action following an incident in the home, then your veterinary surgeon should be called in.

ENTROPION

This is a hereditary condition of the eye, either the upper or the lower eyelids turning inwards, usually the lower. The dog blinks a good deal and the eyes discharge copiously. Surgery is comparatively simple and is usually successful, the eyelids being turned back to their normal position. The condition is more common in breeds which have been bred for a smaller eye than usual.

EPILEPSY

Fits of short duration are not uncommon in small puppies during the course of teething. The youngster's eyes will glaze over, and he may froth a little at the mouth, then keel over. In such instances keep the dog quiet in a warm room until he recovers. More serious fits which are occasioned during the aftermath of a virus disease or due to an accident or some hereditary condition are seldom entirely curable.

EPISTAXIS

Nose bleed. Ice packs on the organ will usually alleviate, even stop the flow quickly. The common cause is a blow on the nose, but if the

---

*A comprehensive list of such plants can be found in: *Poisonous Plants in Britain and their effects on Animals and Man*, HMSO, 1984 and *The Exhibitor's Diary, 1987*, Petcetera, etc. Solihull, 1987.

bleeding persists, the matter should be referred to the veterinary surgeon who will examine the dog for foreign bodies in the nostrils.

EPULIS

This is a hard fibrous growth in the gums, sometimes to be found in veteran dogs. If necessary, it can be removed by surgery, but if the dog does not appear unduly inconvenienced it is better left alone.

GASTRO-ENTERITIS

Diarrhoea, sometimes flecked with blood, is a common symptom, this becoming darker and more blood-stained if allowed to remain untreated, when it can result in death. Stomach pain, vomiting (which is often white and frothy) and loss of weight will be noted and the dog should be put on a very light diet of milky foods, warm bread and milk being particularly good. Raw meat should be withdrawn entirely while the dog is loose in his motions.

HEAT STROKE

A dog left unattended in the rays of a hot sun or penned in the back of a closed vehicle will sometimes collapse from heat-stroke. A dog so thoughtlessly treated should be allowed a limited drink of cold water to which a little salt has been added; then bath the animal gently all over his body with cool water, letting him rest for an hour or two in a well ventilated room.

HERNIA

There are several kinds of hernia conditions. The one usually encountered is the *umbilical* form, shown by a bump on the navel. It is often caused by the dam biting roughly and inexpertly at the umbilical cord when she whelps the puppy. Few veterinary surgeons would consider a small example of this form of hernia an unsoundness. Sometimes these protuberances look a little unsightly when the dog is in puppyhood, they are often insignificant however, when the animal becomes mature. If it is thought necessary to remove one, a veterinary surgeon can effect this quite easily while the dog is in his first year. Home methods which include strapping back the bump for several weeks seldom prove effective and serve only to irritate the dog. Other forms of hernia include the *inguinal* kind, more often experienced by a bitch than a dog. This is seen in a swelling behind the inguinal teats which are situated in the groin. This hernia condition and also the *scrotal*, *diaphragmatic* and *perineal* hernias, the last-named sometimes found in the veteran dog are more serious forms and require professional attention as soon as detected.

HIP DYSPLASIA (HD)

This is a genetic problem involving the degeneration of the *acetatabulum* (hip socket) into which the femoral head (knuckle bone) should easily slide but does not in the case of an affected dog. Fortunately, HD affects Cairn Terriers not at all, and seems confined to the longer-legged, therefore longer-boned breeds. However, this does not mean that a wary and vigilant watch should not be kept for signs of it in individual animals. The disease itself has been known in humans for many centuries and in canines for a comparatively shorter time, but whereas awareness of it in dogs commenced with just a few breeds, now a goodly number are involved and are receiving corrective treatment under a joint scheme managed by the BVA (British Veterinary Association) and the Kennel Club.

It must be remembered that this complex hereditary condition should never be allowed to penetrate Cairn Terriers, hence this brief, cautionary description.

INDIGESTION

This can be caused by eating unsuitable food or eating too much. Stomach pain will be experienced, also bowel noises. Treatment is to give the dog a little stomach powder mixed in warm milk and to stop feeding him for a day or more according to his response. When feeding re-starts ensure that he has sensibly balanced meals in modest quantity.

LICE

Most dogs in their time receive these unwelcome visitors. They cause intense irritation and their eggs, often to be seen attached to the coat, should be picked off and burnt, otherwise they will hatch out in only a few days. The best way to deal with lice is to remove them manually between finger and thumb after causing them to be active with a metal comb teased through the dense coat. Then bathe the dog in a suitable anti-parasite preparation of which there are several good makes on the market. Let it dry on the coat, then brush off, completing the process with an electric dryer and/or towel. There are also some good dusting powders available which will deal effectively with these parasites and they should be used according to the makers' instructions.

MANGE

A common enemy of the dog, this appears in various forms, as wet and dry eczema, 'dermatitis' and parasitic mange. Unless pernicious, most of the forms in which these appear can be dealt with satisfactorily and will clear up nicely, although the time taken in achieving good results can vary from days to months according to the severity of the attack.

Follicular Mange: This seems the common form and at one time it was considered a killer mange, being very difficult to cure. Whole litters became affected and had to be put down. However, thanks now to modern veterinary medicine the condition is reasonably easy to eradicate. The short-coated breeds are more prone to it than say Cairns, but most breeds become involved, nevertheless. Keep a watch out for bareness around the eyes and ears. Bare patches on the hocks and other thin-coat areas should be a warning signal. The parasites burrow into and live in the hair follicles and the patches made usually start off about $\frac{1}{2}$ in (13 mm) in diameter, gradually spreading over the body and sometimes assuming an elephant-grey colour with reddish tints. Occasionally pustular spots form and when erupting emit an unpleasant pungent smell. There are a number of proprietary ointments to be had and the wise breeder takes heed of traditional elixirs which have been found good in the kennels of some old-timers. Veterinary preparations are improving all the time, but it is sensible to ensure that the patient is well exercised and kept in good general health. Often, a change of diet coupled with a course of thyroid gland treatment, which must be prescribed and monitored by your veterinary surgeon, will usually expedite a cure.

Sarcoptic Mange: This is a form of dry eczema and is similar to scabies in humans. It often affects dogs who are ill-kempt and out of condition thus emphasising the necessity for an immediate toning-up course coupled with nutritive feeding. The initial rashes are frequently found on the soft skin of the belly and groins, resembling acne. The skin becomes harsh and dry, the dog's coat begins to stare, then spots appear as the hair falls out. It may prove necessary to try a variety of medicines and ointments to find a cure, but this is a good policy to adopt with all skin complaints as they seem to vary in effect and intensity from dog to dog. It will be found that the average dog's digestive powers are adversely affected and it is important to guard against the patient's general debilitation. The popular ointment among many dog breeders when confronted with mange of this kind is one made from a base of flowers sulphur. This is readily obtainable as are lotions for bathing the dog.

Ringworm: This is an unpleasant and dangerous form as it can be contracted by humans and children must be warned to keep away from an affected dog. It is a fungoid disease and the main causes are bad feeding and overcrowding. The ring-like patches are very contagious and spread from dog to dog in a kennel. It must be treated at once and there are a number of useful remedies to be had.

POISONING

Give the victim an emetic immediately, practical forms being available in the average domestic household. A dessertspoonful of common salt in a quarter pint of water or a similar solution of mustard being particularly effective. A small knob of common soda will work well too. The usual poisons encountered are:

Acids: Antidote: Bicarbonate of soda.

Alkalies: Usually absorbed from household cleansing agents. Antidote: Vinegar or lemon juice.

Arsenic: Antidote: Epsom Salts, lime or barley water, magnesia, egg whites beaten in milk, diluted olive oil, peroxide of iron.

Coal Gas: Antidote: Immediate removal to fresh air, artificial respiration, ammonia to the nostrils, a little brandy orally, hot and cold douches alternately.

Hyrocyanic Acid: Taken as a rule from eating laurel leaves or those of the wild cherry. Antidote: Dextrose or corn syrup.

Iodine: Antidote: Starch and water mixture, arrowroot, cornflower. Morphia and morphine derivatives can be given before and after the emetic.

Lead: Taken from paint pigments, licking painted toys or woodwork etc. Antidotes: whites of eggs beaten in milk, milk of magnesia, Epsom Salts (a dessertspoonful in about quarter-pint of warm water), dilute sulphuric acid or potassium iodide. High saline irrigation is important.

Mercury: Taken by licking skin ointments, thereby absorbing bichloride of mercury, or coal tar derivatives from mange lotions or rat poison. Antidote: whites of eggs beaten in milk or water (before and after the emetic), gluten of wheat.

Phosphorus: Taken by puppies playing with and eating matches or by dogs eating baits set for rats. Antidote: Refrain from giving oily or fatty substances, even creamy milk, as these increase the solubility of the poison. Give three to five grains of copper sulphate or permanganate of potash every twenty minutes until the veterinary surgeon arrives. Epsom Salts are effective too.

Strychnine: The common medium of dog poisoners, very effective and rapid. Can be taken by a dog eating bones of rats, etc themselves poisoned by eating strychnine which lasts in their bones for many years. Antidote: Best is an injection of apomorphia, others being chloral hydrate and amyl nitrate – these must be given by the veterinary surgeon. First aid must be given in the form of an immediate emetic, also by giving patient butter, dripping and other fats. Keep in a dark room meanwhile.

Finally, it is as well to observe caution when giving laxatives. Many of these contain strychnine and an overdose of laxatives can prove fatal to a dog in the small breeds. Violent purges, notably those intended for humans are quite unsuitable for dogs. Any dog so dosed and evincing symptoms of poisoning may require morphia or apomorphine hydrochloride injected subcutaneously.

If you have a chance of establishing which poison was taken by your dog before you telephone for veterinary assistance, mention your suspicions to your veterinary surgeon prior to his arrival so that he can come prepared.

ROUNDWORM

Few dogs escape infestation from the common roundworm. It usually becomes necessary to dispose of worms in young puppies and today this is a simple job which can be done without utilising the old system of starving the subject first. There are many veterinary preparations available, all of them good, or your veterinary surgeon will attend to the matter for you. Unless this is done, an infested puppy will never thrive and may become an easy victim to any canine disease which besets him. It is common practice to treat a bitch for possible worms before breeding with her. The process can do no harm even assuming she is free from them at the time. It may also save heavy infestation in her young. Care should be taken to disinfect regularly puppies' quarters, coupled with frequent washing. When the worms are emitted they will come through either the puppy's mouth or its anus. Vermicilli-like in their appearance and usually in a tight skein they should be shovelled up and burnt at once. It is best to wait until the puppy is at least five weeks old before worming him. The process should not take place until weaning has been commenced and is well under way – six weeks of age being a generally considered good time to do it. However, if the youngster is so bloated with worms as to necessitate worming earlier, say at four weeks or younger, then a veterinary surgeon should be asked to act in the matter.

RUPTURE (*See* Hernia)

STINGS

Wasps and bees are the main offenders and their stings can be serious, although an isolated sting can be easily dealt with as a rule. Dogs are liable to snap at and trap these insects in their mouths, so in and around the mouth is the usual place for stings to occur. The foot is another commonly affected place for stings to be received, especially in late summer when stinging insects are lethargic and are pawed at. Dab on at once a strong solution of antiseptic or bathe around the sting (after extracting the barb) with a strong bicarbonate of soda and water mixture (two tablespoonfuls well stirred into a pint of water). If the sting is on the foot, stand the member in a shallow bowl of the same solution or rub the sting with a lump of common washing soda.

TAPEWORM

An unpleasant parasite which is said to be passed on by the flea and/or by eating rabbit. As its name suggests it is like a length of narrow, creamy coloured tape composed of segments which on their own look like fat grains of rice. The presence of a tapeworm can sometimes be revealed by one or more of the segments adhering to the dog's anal region or in his stool. Care should be taken to ensure that other dogs in the kennel area do not come into contact with infected stools and the ground around should be systematically swabbed down with a disinfectant twice daily. The victim of tapeworm will become depressed, lose weight and evince no interest in food, although it has been found that the opposite symptom has been encountered at times. The worm can be expelled with modern veterinary drugs. Often, they are found to be many feet in length and a dog so cleared of this scourge will immediately pick up in health and begin to thrive.

TOXOCARA CANIS INFECTION

This disease is a dangerous one for it can extend to children. In 1987 a joint statement by the British Medical Association and the British Veterinary Association on the disease included a recommendation that dogs should be excluded from areas in parks designated as children's play areas. The BVA's Public Health Committee has expressed concern that the recommendation may lead to abuse by some authorities extending large areas of parks or recreation fields to play areas beyond existing sites.

The disease comes from the larvae of the ordinary roundworm usually found in breeding bitches and whelps. Broadly speaking, the round-worm lays its sticky eggs which are passed out of the puppy via its faeces. These eggs adhere to the youngsters' anal region also to its box or bedding. A child handling the puppy may well get some on its skin. The larvae which results could enter the child's body through its skin, which it has to pierce. A very remote chance exists that the larvae could reach behind the child's eyes, damaging its sight.

The danger period in the matter ranges from two months of age to a year when the worm is believed ineffective. It will be seen, nevertheless, how important it is to worm young stock for roundworm. Puppies should be conscientiously wormed at six, ten, twelve weeks, then at nine months. A brood bitch, assumed to be in whelp, should be wormed seven days following her mating.

Acupuncture

Although it must be admitted that I cannot claim experience in veterinary acupuncture, reports of its success in certain instances are frequent. Mostly, it seems, good results come from professional treatment of prolapsed introvertabral disc conditions (P.I.D. or 'slipped disc'). Muscle sprains and strains seems to respond well to this method. Arthritis and minor conditions involving paralysis have also been treated with varying degrees of success; a lot depends, of course, on how advanced are the symptoms at the outset.

It is important to remember that cures cannot be accomplished 'in a day'. A course of regular treatment has to be faced, probably entailing visits to the centre over several months with booster treatment every year in order that improvements are kept under control.

It seems unnecessary to emphasise to dog owners contemplating a course of acupuncture for their dogs to ensure they take the patient to a fully qualified veterinary acupuncturist and preferably one with established successes in that art as well as in orthodox veterinary medicine and surgery.

8 Glossary of Terms and Points

Beginners, especially, are sometimes confused by the host of descriptive and semi-technical words they encounter in dogs. These are more evident perhaps, in dog show critiques and fanciers' discussion meetings. The parlance is quite extensive, many of the words used being more appropriate to specific breeds, the word 'Harlequin' for example (not included in this Glossary) being virtually confined to Great Danes as a coat marking description, whereas 'hard-mouthed' and 'gun-shy' are terms which apply to the retrieving and field breeds such as the Spaniels and other gundogs, when applicable. Some terms are in general use throughout dogdom, and the picturesque 'cow-hocks', 'in-toed' and 'camel back' indicate faults in most known breeds. Fig. 2 on page 28 can be used in reference to various terms in the Glossary.

AFFIX: A name granted by the Kennel Club General Committee to a breeder allowing him the sole right to use such Affix as part of a name when registering or changing the name of a dog. Where the Grantee of a registered Affix wishes to use it when naming a dog bred by him or which was bred from parents which were bred by him, then the Affix must be used as a prefix (as the first word of a dog's name). Otherwise it must be used as a suffix (the last word of a dog's name).

ANGULATION: A term used to describe relationship or the angle made by bones when forming joints, generally directed to haunch-bone, tibia and femur in the hindlimbs and shoulder bone, radius and humerus in the forelimbs. Poor angulation suggests obtuse, therefore weak formation; good angulation infers satisfactory coordination of the bones.

ANORCHID: A male dog without testicles, and unable to procreate. Can be confused with cryptorchidism, although it is a rare condition.

APPLE HEAD: Rounded (like an apple) on top of the skull. Seen in the Toy Spaniel, but undesirable in many breeds.

A.V. (A.O.V.): Any Variety/Any Other Variety: A show term found in Definition of Classes indicating that different varieties or breeds are eligible for competition.

BACK-CROSSING: To breed a cross-bred dog or bitch back to one of its parents or to a dog of the same breed as one of its parents.

BAD-DOER: A dog who does not thrive in spite of good care and attention. Such dogs are seldom good feeders and are fastidious even from puppyhood.

BALANCE: When seen in profile, from the front also the rear, the dog's outline should be pleasing, without exaggeration and evenly conformed as required by the breed Standard. The picture should be maintained to give stylish and sound action when moved both ways.

BARREL: Referring to the ribs, the cage of which should be well sprung and rounded, akin in some ways to a barrel. The term is used rather to emphasise the necessity for ample lung room.

B.B./B.O.B.: An abbreviation for Best of Breed.

BEEFY: Coarseness, especially in the region of the hindquarters.

BITCHY: Disparaging term applied to a male dog with feminine lines and expression.

BITE: Refers to relative position of upper and lower incisors of the forward jaw when closed. See: OVERSHOT, UNDERSHOT, WRY MOUTH, etc.

BLOCKY: Stocky, either in head or body.

BLOOM: Physical well-being evinced by glossy coat.

BONE: A dog with ample bone is one normally well-endowed structurally, the limbs especially having the feel of strength and spring. A dog with poor bone may lack calcium, one with too much bone evince coarseness.

BRACE: Two dogs of the same breed or two exhibited together in the Brace Class.

BREEDER: (or Br: abbreviation): The legal owner of a bitch at the time she whelps.

BRISKET: The part of the dog's body in front of the chest and between the forelegs.

BROOD BITCH: A bitch kept solely for breeding use. Such an animal should be strong, typical and sound both temperamentally and physically.

B.S./B.I.S.: Best in Show.

BUTTERFLY NOSE: When the nostrils show flesh coloured patches with the black pigment.

CAMEL BACK: Another name for Roach Back.

CAT FOOT: A compact, round foot which is well arched as in the cat.

C.C.: Challenge Certificate. A Cairn needs to win three Challenge Certificates, each under a different judge at a different championship show held under Kennel Club Rules and Regulations to become a Show Champion. This applies to shows in Great Britain.

C.D.: Companion Dog. A title gained by a dog who has passed a test in

Obedience. C.D.X.=Companion Dog (Excellent). A superior award in Obedience work.

CH./CHAMPION: See: CHALLENGE CERTIFICATE.

CHEEKY: Abnormal fullness of the cheek muscles.

CHEST: The forepart of the body enclosed by the ribs.

CHOPS: Pendulous lips.

CLODDY: Thick-set build.

CLOSE-COUPLED: Well put together and short from last rib-bone to haunch-bone.

COBBY: Compact and close-coupled.

CONDITION: Refers to health, physical and temperamental, coat and general bloom.

CONFORMATION: The form, outline, structural perfection and physical features of the breed according to its Standard.

CORKY: Lively, perky and active with good type.

COUPLINGS: See: WELL-COUPLED.

COUPLE: Two of a breed.

COW-HOCKED: When the points of hocks turn in towards each other, thereby turning out the rear feet. A fault.

CREST: The arched upper sections of the neck.

CROUP: The region which abounds the sacrum down to set-on of the tail.

CROWN: Highest part of the skull.

CRYPTORCHID: A male dog whose testicles have not descended in the scrotum. A dog in this state will be unable to procreate, neither can he compete in exhibition under Kennel Club Rules.

DAM: The mother of puppies, the term being used from the time she whelps them.

DEW-CLAWS: A fifth claw with little or no purpose to be found on the inside of front legs and sometimes found on hind limbs. These should be removed a few days after birth by the veterinary surgeon.

DEWLAP: The loose skin below the throat.

DOGGY: Disparaging term applied to a bitch with male lines and expression.

DOME: Refers to rounded skull.

DOWN IN PASTERN: Sagging or weakness in the lowest part of legs between knee (or hock) and foot.

DUAL CHAMPION: A dog who has qualified for not only Show Champion status, but qualified for a Working Certificate in the Field.

ELBOW: Joint at the top of the forearm. The elbows should be close to the body and the points of elbow should never turn out. When they do, this is referred to as 'out at elbow' and is a fault.

ENTIRETY: A dog is said to be entire when both the testicles are descended in the scrotum.

EXPRESSION: An outlook, typical of the breed, composed of and formed by size, colour, positioning of the eyes coupled with the use of the ears.

FEATHER: The fringe of hair which adorns the back of a Cairn's legs. The term can include fringing on ears and tail.

FIELD TRIAL: Competition in the field, the dogs being judged on their aptitude with game.

FRILL: Hair under the neck and on chest.

FURNISHED: Mature, developed in full.

GAIT: Mode of action, style of movement.

GENES: Units of inheritance, emanating from both parents.

GESTATION: The period of time from conception to birth of the puppies, usually nine weeks or sixty-three days.

GOOD-DOER: A dog who thrives well naturally, always seeming to be in good bloom and eating well.

GOOSE-RUMP: A croup which slopes down too abruptly, the tail seemingly set on too low.

GUN-SHY: A dog who fears the gun and its report.

HANDLER: A person who handles a dog whether in Exhibition, Obedience or Working duties.

HARE-FEET: Feet which are rather long and narrow, the digits splayed as in the hare.

HAUNCH: Region immediately above hip joint.

HAW: Excessive drop or hang of the inner lid of the eye, usually showing bloodshot.

H.C.: Highly Commended. Sixth award placing in exhibition, but normally with no cash value.

HEAT: Season, Period or Oestrum. When the bitch is menstruating.

HOCKS: Equivalent to the ankle in humans. The joints between the pasterns and stifle in hind legs.

HUCKLE BONES: The top of the hip joints.

HUMERUS: The arm-bone. This articulates with lower end of shoulder blade, being slightly curved and lying obliquely to join with radius and ulna to form the elbow joint.

IN-BREEDING: The planned mating of close relatives such as father to daughter, etc. in order to 'fix' certain desirable points, already existing in the mating pair and their background.

INTERNATIONAL CHAMPION/INT. CH.: A dog who has gained the title of champion in more than one country. Officially, this title is not recognised by the English Kennel Club.

LEATHER: The skin of the ear-flap. Widely used to include the ear itself.

LEGGY: Too tall on the leg as to make the dog unbalanced.

LEVEL JAWS: When the upper incisors rest over and upon the lower incisors with no apparent space between them. This is the correct mouth formation in the Cairn Terrier.

LIGHT EYE: Eyes which are amber or light in colour.

LINE-BREEDING: The planned mating of a dog or bitch with his or her relatives from strains which are similar although not too close. It is common to mate dogs with the same sire and different dams and vice versa, but it is essential that the mating pair are good specimens and closely resemble each other.

LIPPY: Abnormal development of the lips causing them to overhang.

LITTER: Term given to the family of puppies born to the bitch at one time.

LITTER CLASSES: Classes arranged at some dog shows for litters which are not older than three months or younger than six weeks on the show date.

LOADED AT SHOULDER: When the shoulder muscles are over-developed giving an impression of heaviness.

LOIN: Region on either side of vertebral column between last ribs and hindquarters.

LONG CAST: Opposite to short-coupled, similar to long-coupled, i.e. long in back and couplings, particularly with reference to the distance between last rib and hip joint.

LOW SET: Refers usually to a tail which is set on low, but can refer to a dog rather short in the leg, or ears which are set on low to the head.

LUMBER: Overweight in flesh and timber making the dog ungainly.

MAIDEN: A bitch which has not had puppies. In show classification a class open to exhibits which have never won a first prize.

MANTLE: Refers to the darker part of the coat on shoulders, sides and back.

MASK: Dark markings on the muzzle or the muzzle itself.

MATCH: Competition conducted under Kennel Club Rules and Regulations between pairs of dogs of the same or different breeds, a system of elimination being used until final winner is found.

MATRON: Refers to a brood bitch.

MISSING: When a bitch fails to conceive in spite of the fact that the mating was satisfactory and that both animals in the union were normal.

MONORCHID: A male dog with only one testicle descended in the scrotum.

MUZZLE: That part of the headpiece which comprises the foreface, including jaw, nose and lips. Could also refer to a contraption of straps or wire used to stop a dog biting.

N.A.F.: Name Applied For. Indicates that the dog's owner has applied to the Kennel Club to register his dog with a given name.

N.F.C.: Not For Competition. A show term indicating that the exhibit is at the show for display and not for competition.

NOVICE: A beginner in the dog game. In show classification a class open to exhibits who have not won three or more first prizes.

OCCIPUT: The bone at the top of the back of the skull. Although prominent in some Hounds and the old type of Field Spaniel it should not be too evident in Terrier varieties.

OESTRUM: The bitch's menstrual period, sometimes referred to as the 'season', 'heat' or 'showing colour'.

OPEN SHOW: A show held under Kennel Club Rules and Regulations and open to all breeds with no challenge certificates on offer.

OUT AT ELBOW: When the points of elbow turn out and away from the wall of chest. A fault.

OUT AT SHOULDER: When shoulders protrude outwards and loosely, giving an impression of width when viewed from the front. A fault.

OUT-BREEDING or OUT-CROSSING: The mating of entirely unrelated dogs.

OVERHANG: Term given to heaviness or protrusion of the brow.

OVERSHOT: When the upper incisors project thereby making a space between them and the lower incisors. Sometimes known as 'pig-jaw'.

PADS: The cushioned soles of the feet.

PASTERN: That part of the leg below the knee on the forelimbs and below hock in the hindlimbs.

PEDIGREE: The dog's 'family tree' showing his sire and dam and the names of his ancestry usually taken back to three or four generations.

PIGEON-CHESTED: When the sternum or breastbone projects abnormally.

PIGEON-TOED: Sometimes referred to as In-toed. When the toes turn in or point towards each other. A cow-hocked dog is often pigeon-toed as is one who is out at elbow.

PIG-EYED: Eyes which are small and close-lidded.

PIG-JAW: See: OVERSHOT.

PILE: Dense or thick undercoat of a long-coated dog.

PLAITING: Manner of walking or trotting, in which the legs cross.

POINTS: Can refer to the anatomical points detailed by the breed Standard or to nails, lips, eye-rims, nose.

PRICK-EARS: Ears which are carried erect as in a Bull-Terrier.

PUPPY: In law, a dog up to the age of six months, but the Kennel Club treat him as a puppy up to one year of age.

QUALITY: Refinement with Type.

QUARTERS: The fore-parts (fore-quarters) and hind-parts (hind-quarters). The term is usually applied to the latter.

RACY: A dog who although quite well developed is inclined to unusual length and reach.

RANGY: A long-bodied, rather leggy specimen, lacking depth.

RAT-TAIL: A well-rooted tail tapering to a tip and covered with short-hair, like a rat's.

RESERVE: The fourth place in show awards, usually without monetary value.

RIBBED UP: Long ribs.

RINGER: A substitute for a dog of similar appearance to another.

ROACH BACK: When the spine arches upwards from the withers towards the loin.

RUFF: Long hair standing out from the neck.

RUNNING ON: A doggy term which refers to keeping a promising puppy for several months to ascertain his ultimate worth as a show prospect.

RUNT: Undersized, poorest puppy in a litter.

SANCTION SHOW: A show held under Kennel Club Rules and Regulations and confined to members of a canine society, and subjected to special sanction.

SCAPULA: The shoulder blade.

SEASON: See: OESTRUM.

SECOND TEETH: The permanent teeth which replace the first mouth or puppy teeth.

SECOND THIGH: The part of the hind leg which extends from stifle to the hock.

SELF-COLOUR: One colour coat. Sometimes referred to as self-marked.

SEPTUM: The vertical dividing line between the nostrils.

SERVICE: Term used in mating when the dog 'covers' the bitch, i.e. the act of copulation.

SET-ON: Usually refers to where the tail joins the body.

SHELLY: Term used to describe a shallow, ill-developed body.

SHORT-COUPLED: Short in back and loins.

SICKLE-HOCKS: Hocks which are well bent and nicely let down.

SICKLE-TAIL: A tail which is formed like a sickle and carried out and up.

SILENT HEAT: When evidence of oestrum is unseen, i.e. no coloured discharge, in spite of the bitch being ready for mating. Probably due to a hormone deficiency.

SIRE: The male parent.

SLAB-SIDED: Flat-ribbed.

SNIPY: Refers to a muzzle which is pointed and weak.

SOUNDNESS: A dog is said to be sound when he is in good health physically and mentally and is normal throughout.

SPAYED: A bitch is said to be spayed when her ovaries have been removed surgically, so that she becomes incapable of having puppies.

SPEAK: To bark.

SPREAD: The distance between the forelegs, i.e. width of front.

SPRING: Refers to the elasticity of the rib cage.

STANCE: Posture.

STANDARD: The official description or word picture of the perfect Cairn Terrier drawn up originally by a panel of breed experts and approved by the Kennel Club.

STERN: Tail of a sporting dog.

STILTED: Refers to mincing gait, usually due to upright shoulder emplacement.

STOP: Depression between and in front of the eyes, similar to bridge of the nose in humans.

STRAIGHT IN HOCK: A hock which is almost vertical, lacking bend.

STRAIN: A family or clan of dogs with a distinct bloodline which has stemmed from notable dogs in the past.

STUD: A stud dog or where stud dogs are kept. A dog kept and used for servicing bitches whose owners will pay a nominal fee for his use.

SUBSTANCE: Good substance suggests ample bone and physical development.

SWAY BACK: A dip behind the shoulders at the withers, showing poor muscular development.

T.A.F.: Transfer Applied For. The letters to be put after a dog's name on the show entry form when a new owner has not by that date received official notice of transfer of ownership to his name.

TEAM: Three or more dogs of one breed or variety.

THROATINESS: With surplus and loose skin under the throat.

TICKING: Small flecks of dark hair on a white coat.

TIE: When the mating pair become 'tied' tail to tail while copulation takes place.

TIMBER: Substance and bone.

TOPLINE: The line of the back when the dog is viewed in profile.

TUCKED-UP: Term applied to posture of dog when his stomach muscles are contracted, either when in pain or naturally according to his breed if say, a dog of the chase, such as Greyhound, Whippet, Borzoi.

TYPE: The qualities characteristic of an individual breed to make him a model of his variety.

TYRO: Beginner or Novice.

UMBILICAL CORD: The cord joining the unborn puppy to the placenta.

UNDERCOAT: Dense, soft and short weather resistant coat beneath the top coat.

UNDERSHOT: When the lower incisors project beyond the upper incisors when the mouth is closed.

UNSOUND: A dog which is unfit either physically, mentally or both. Unsoundness can be inherited or acquired temporarily (such as a broken leg). Anything which causes the dog to fail in function such as in movement, working aptitude etc. can be termed an unsoundness.

UPRIGHT SHOULDER: When the shoulder blade and upper arm joint makes an obtuse angle, causing stilted action.

UPSWEEP: Seen in an undershot specimen when lower jaw sweeps up and out.

VENT: The anal region, sometimes used in reference to the anus.

VETERAN CLASS: A class at dog shows usually for exhibits of seven years and over.

V.H.C.: Very Highly Commended. An award at dog shows fifth in order of merit.

WALL EYE: A term which encompasses the china blue and pearl eye colours, associated with a merle coat.

WEAVING: A form of movement when the dog crosses his front legs one over the other.

WEEDY: Lacking substance and bone.

WELL-LET-DOWN: Refers to hocks which are short and which make good angulation at the joint.

WELL SPRUNG: Refers to ribs which are nicely rounded and elastic.

WHEEL-BACK: A back which is arched from withers over the loins to the hips.

WHELPS: Puppies are termed thus from birth until they open their eyes about ten days later.

WHOLE COLOUR: Self or one coloured coat.

WITHERS: The top of the shoulder blades at the base of the neck.

WORKING CERTIFICATE: A certificate awarded at Field Trials to gundogs who have qualified in working trials and general breed duties. A Show Champion receiving such an award is entitled to the title of Dual Champion.

WRINKLE: Loose skin or folds of skin on foreface and brow.

WRY MOUTH: When the incisors of top jaw cross at one point the incisors of the lower jaw. The worst form of mouth formation incapable of making a clean bite.

Appendix 1

Breed clubs and their secretaries

NOTE: While the names and addresses given here have been checked at time of proofing this book, they cannot be guaranteed as correct indefinitely owing to the frequent changes in conditions.

Cairn Terrier Association: Mrs B. Dewhurst, 68 Rosehill Road, Burnley, Lancashire BB11 2QX (0282) 35491

Cairn Terrier Club: Mr J. A. Berrecloth, 6 Duff Street, Dundee, Scotland DN4 7AN (0382) 42931

Midland Cairn Terrier Club: Mrs L. Firth, 1A Columbia Avenue, Sutton-in-Ashfield, Nottinghamshire NG17 2GZ (0623) 512621

North of Ireland Cairn Terrier Club: Mr J. Dean, 19 Terryhoogan Road, Scarva, Craighaven, Co. Armagh, Northern Ireland BT63 6NF (0762) 831458

Southern Cairn Terrier Club: Mrs M. Towers, Turnagain Lodge, Hook Green, Wilmington, Kent DA2 7AJ (0322) 25191

South Wales and West of England Cairn Terrier Club: Mr J. Radford, 1 Chapel Rise, Atworth, Melkesham, Wiltshire SN12 8JZ (0225) 703865

Dog journals, breed correspondents and contributors

Dog World 9 Tufton Street, Ashford, Kent (0233) 22389

Mr E. Loader, 2 North End Lane, Malvern, Worcestershire RW14 2ES (0684) 568722

Miss J. M. Hudson, 7 Hirstead Road, Newby, Scarborough, Yorkshire (0723) 65284

Our Dogs Publishing Co. Ltd., 5 Oxford Road Station Approach, Manchester M60 1SX (061) 236 2660

Mr Frank Hayward, Moorefield, Goosnargh Lane, Goosnargh, Preston, Lancashire PR3 2BM (0772) 865377

Mrs M. Shuttleworth, 16 Frederick Avenue, Hinckley, Leicestershire (0455) 611813

The Cairn Terrier Club

Although this club was formed 'in spirit' if not in deed in 1909 it was not until one year later that it actually came into working being; the very first specialist breed club for the Cairn Terrier which had recently been nominated thus following a spell when they were known as 'short-coated prick-eared Skye Terriers' a nondescript, unimpressive title which was well dispensed with. The formation of the club was in Edinburgh at the North British Hotel with Allan McDonald president and Mrs Alastair Campbell hon. secretary, some fifty-four members forming the nucleus of membership at the time, these mostly from Scotland. It is interesting to note that in the club's constitution is the requirement that the secretary or president should be resident in Scotland during their term of office. The club arranged shows for the 'new' breed following the drawing-up of its Standard in 1911 and much progress was made in the promotion of the breed's image throughout the land. Unfortunately, present-day historians are at considerable disadvantage in formulating a detailed picture of the club's progress and procedures during the period which led up to the Great War because the records for that important era in the club's life have been lost. However, it is known that the club held a championship show in 1930, some eighteen years after the first issue of Challenge Certificates to Cairns in 1912 at Richmond Championship Show when Mrs Alastair Campbell judged. The Prince of Wales became Patron of the Cairn Terrier Club in 1924 but with the missing documentation, we are unable to report in detail what must have held consumate interest to breed students. Suffice to say, the Cairn Terrier Club 'started it off' and with the passing of seven decades and more can claim to have educated dogdom to the worth of the Cairn Terrier and to have formed the nucleus of a worldwide prosperity for the breed. The club's influence is not a localised one like some who work in established geographical areas, but it has been developed purposefully along the lines of a true Parent Club. Its officers over the half century include Lt. Col. Whitehead who had control as secretary and treasurer from 1926 to 1938 then from 1946 to 1964. Much of what we know about the history in those years comes from his written works. However, the presidents in office have been:

1910– Allan McDonald	–1928 Mr J. Wallace	1929–1962 Baroness Burton	1962–1969 Mrs M. Buchanan
1969–1977 Miss E. M. Luis	–1985 Mr W. McCulloch		

and hon. secretaries

1910–1919 Mrs A. Campbell	1919–1926 Major I. Ewing	1926–1938 Lt. Col. H. Whitehead	1938–1946 Dr J. N. Pickard
1946–1964 Lt. Col. H. Whitehead	1966–1967 Major G. Stewart	1967–1976 Mr T. A. Hogg	1976–1980 Mrs M. E. McKinlay
1980–date John A. Berrecloth			

The club issues its annual *Year Book* which is eagerly looked forward to by all breeders and fanciers. The club's honorary secretary is the well-known and popular John Berrecloth.

The Midland Cairn Terrier Club

Although this club's initial application for recognition in March 1980 was fraught with much disappointment when the Kennel Club refused permission, an appeal was later lodged in the August of the same year. This was supported with many letters from prominent breed people. Although the original application which had been published in the *Kennel Gazette* (April 1980) had incited a number of objections at the time, the Kennel Club now agreed that the application could be channelled forward, but that the new club's activities would have to be confined to five adjacent counties, naming them as Derbys., Leics., Lincs., Northants, and Notts.

The Kennel Club finally approved a revised application on 22 January 1981 following an inaugural meeting by enthusiasts at Annesley, Leics. on 26 October 1980. The meeting was chaired by the late W. N. Bradshaw of the 'Redletter' Cairns, who in the year following formation was made hon. life vice-president of the club. No other club had been formed in the breed since 1925 and it was at once well-supported. Today, the Midland Cairn Terrier Club is in a very strong position, bot numerically and financially. Mrs Linda Firth ('Cairngold') is the hon. secretary and Mr A. V. Price is president with Alan Firth treasurer. The committee of twelve is chaired by Jack Watson. Newsletters prove very popular, these are edited by Mrs M. Jennings and a first *Year Book* was issued in 1986.

The North of Ireland Cairn Terrier Club

Probably due to its geographical position, this is the smallest of the Cairn specialist clubs, but the enthusiasm which permeates its membership is immense and major shows scheduling Cairn classes which at one time had to be guaranteed by the club no longer call for support as the breed classes get well filled. The club at the present time does limit its support with guarantees to Open shows where the classes come under a Cairn specialist judge. The club was formed in 1930 by exhibitors anxious to develop their breed. Following World War II the club's membership had built up to over sixty active exhibitors, but mainly due to political unrest, membership fell, predictably, to almost disastrous figures. However, a united front to the problem was set up, headed by Mr T. A. Hogg, then secretary of the Cairn Terrier Club. His life-saving aid was acknowledged by the N.I.C.T.C. by making him vice-president in 1981 and later the club's first hon. life vice-president in 1983. In 1981 the first *Year Book* was published, also the first Open Show staged. Championship status was granted by the Kennel Club and the club's first Championship event was held in the McNeill Hall in Larne in March 1982. Members from the other British clubs prove great supporters at the shows and a first-class bond of unity exists between them all. The hon. life president has been connected with the club since its inception and Mrs D. Walmsley, one time its president, is now the hon. secretary and manages its affairs with zest and experience.

The Southern Cairn Terrier Club

It is believed this long-established club goes back to 1914 which puts it next in age seniority to the Cairn Terrier Club. Then in 1925 when there was a 'breakaway' movement of certain members to form the Cairn Terrier Association, Cairn politics and general activities covered most of England and Scotland. In effect, the S.C.T.C. dealt with activities in the south, the C.T.A. the north of England and the C.T.C. located in Scottish territory. All three dealt with overseas enquiries from time to time. The Southern C.T.C. had Miss Constance Viccars ('Mercia') as secretary who stayed in the post up to 1918 when she and Mrs Dixon acted jointly in the position, the latter lady taking over until 1932 when Mrs Maud Prichard ('Donnington') became secretary and kept in office for twenty-five years. From 1958 to 1964 Mr Alex Fisher, author with J. W. H. Benyon of *The Cairn Terrier*, proved a valuable executive as secretary. Alex Fisher's carefully compiled data on Cairns and Cairn lines have proved to be of inestimable value to the breed. His dossiers were bequeathed to the three clubs on his death, with the S.C.T.C. responsible for them. The late Peggy Wilson ('Felshott') continued their recording as Breed Historian, a post now ably maintained by Bunty Proudlock ('Selkirk'). Sadly, Peggy passed away in April, 1987. Mrs Hilda Manley ('Lofthouse') took over the secretaryship until 1972, followed by Frank Edwards, then by Mrs M. Grey and finally by Mrs Mary Towers ('Deneland') in whose capable hands it remains today. The club's presidents have been noted breeders with Mrs M. Drummond ('Blencathra'), Mrs A. Callaghan, who held office for a year each, then with an extended period to three years. Mrs D. Hamilton ('Oudenarde') and Mrs C. H. Dixon have both been presidents with Miss F. A. Hamilton the president at the present time.

The S.C.T.C. was the first club to hold a breed championship show, and a breed open show in 1952. The membership is quite considerable being around five hundred, which includes a goodly number of overseas enthusiasts. Many functions and meetings are organised and a lot of get-togethers are always on the agenda.

The South Wales and West of England Cairn Terrier Club

With such a progressive breed it became apparent that a club to cater for it in the south-west was necessary. The region had a goodly number of Cairn owners and although very keen and eager to show their dogs, journeying long distances for shows other than championship events was not always a possibility for many. At a Match in Gloucestershire in June, 1980 organised by the S.C.T.C. enthusiasm reached a point where it was decided to form a club for the area. Although the senior clubs evinced some reservations in the plan because they knew little of the local members, an application was made to the Kennel Club to form the South Wales and Border Counties Cairn Terrier Club. The Kennel Club refused to accept the application and it was not until nearly a year later that, on 16 May 1981, an inaugural meeting of prospective members was held in

Chepstow's Two Rivers Hotel and with an attendance of some forty persons present it was opened officially by the late Mr Dean. Officers and Committee were duly elected and with a list of over one hundred names it was decided to appeal to the Kennel Club that the club be admitted to the register of recognised clubs. With the strength of such adequate numbers and now with the backing of the two established clubs, the C.T.C. and C.T.A. whose approval of the appointed executive body was agreed, formal appeal was lodged with the K.C. This was responded to by the Kennel Club who suggested the omission of Border Counties in the proposed title which should be read as South Wales and West of England Cairn Terrier Club. The members accepted this and duly informed the Kennel Club, who at their following meeting in London gave approval to the application and added the club's title to their list of registered clubs – with one proviso, *viz* that the County of Gloucestershire be removed from the new club's field of operations.

The well-known and popular Mr Trevor Evans, a Builth Wells solicitor and Cairn breeder who had originally instigated the idea of a regional club was invited to the chair. Mrs A. S. Dean was voted hon. secretary with her husband as assistant secretary. Mr Graham Peers became hon. treasurer, Mrs J. Parker-Tucker was unanimously voted in as president and both Mrs H. Small and Mrs A. Loader vice-presidents. The club is now, as the breed knows, a highly active and successful body and looking after the interests of all Cairn fanciers in the region. The current hon. secretary is Mr J. Radford ('Skimmerdale') who is editor of the excellent *Cairn '85* publication produced by Graham Peers ('Tweed isle') an active club member.

The Cairn Terrier Association

This association was formed in 1926 following a breakaway movement from the southern club in the previous year. The first secretary to the new body was the Rev T. W. L. Caspersz who set the foundation stone upon which the association's later successes were to be built. He had a strong committee of noted names in the Cairn world, Hawke, Mirlees ('Shinnel'), Fleming ('Out of the West'), Allen, Howard and Johnson ('Keycol'). This was the first breed club to hold a specialist breed show and the first to be granted championship show status. Lady Muriel Worthington was its first president, followed by the Hon. Mary Hawke ('Lockyers'), Mrs M. Bassett ('Frimley'), Mr T. W. L. Caspersz ('Turfield'), Lt. Col. Hector Whitehead ('Guynash'), Mrs Chas. Howard, Mr G. J. Ross ('Firring'), Mrs K. L. Stephen ('Hyver'), Miss C. Viccars ('Mercia') and Major H. A. Townley ('Carysfort'). These were followed by the Baroness Burton ('Dochfour'), again Hector Whitehead and Lady Howard, then Miss J. V. Bengough ('Twobees') who remained until 1961. Mrs Leverton ('Mer-rymeet') was the next president followed by Alex Fisher ('Fimor'), whose records on the breed have proved of inestimable value to the fancy. Mrs Caspersz resigned in 1929 and Major Townley M.B.E. took over until he retired in 1936 with Mr E. V. Wilding-Jones doing some good work for the C.T.A.

over a few years until Major Townley returned to the office again. Then, the inestimable Mrs G. F. Hamilton ('Oudenarde') took the reins from 1945 to 1971 and the C.T.A.'s shows were run at provincial centres as well as in the south; a move which was appreciated by the breed generally. The association today boasts many veteran breeders, some of whom have their connections from as far back as the thirties; these include Mesdames Small ('Avenelhouse'), Strachan, Breach, Tysoe, Heery ('Wimpas'), Sparrow-Wilkinson, Parker-Tucker ('Uniquecottage'), Phillips, Foster-Ring and Mr and Mrs Frank Hayward. Miss M. S. Churchill is chairman and the late Miss M. D. 'Peggy' Wilson ('Felshott'), at one time breed historian was, until her recent death, engaged in keeping a watchful eye on breed activities and contributing to her breed column notes.

The present secretary is Mrs B. Dewhurst who has officiated as honorary treasurer to the C.T.A. since 1972.

The Cairn Terrier Breeders' Code of Ethics

The Cairn Terrier fraternity have established a highly commendable code of ethics which is approved by all the breed clubs and is indicative of the standards adopted in this fine breed. It is as follows:

1 Before breeding a litter, equal weight should be given to type, temperament, health and soundness. Nervous or aggressive dogs are not satisfactory as pets or breeding stock.
2 No bitch should be required to have an excessive number of litters, and no bitch should be mated at every season without regard to the well-being of the bitch.
3 All breeding should be aimed at the improvement of the breed. Members should do all in their power to discourage breeding from clearly inferior specimens, and those members who own stud dogs should refuse stud service to such specimens.
4 No members should breed a litter unless he has time and facilities to devote proper care and attention to the rearing of the puppies and the well-being of the dam, and no member should provide stud service unless he is satisfied that the owner of the bitch has such time and facilities.
5 No member should breed a litter unless he is reasonably sure of finding homes for the puppies. No puppies should leave the breeder before the age of eight weeks.
6 No puppies should be exported before they are fully inoculated or before the age of three months, unless they are travelling in the personal care of the owner or his known representative.
7 No puppies should be sold to countries where they are not protected by anti-cruelty laws. (If in doubt consult the Ministry of Agriculture, R.S.P.C.A., or the Kennel Club.)
8 No puppies should knowingly be sold to laboratories, pet shops or dealers in

dogs, or persons known to sell puppies to any of the above. Nor should stud services be provided for such persons. (A dealer is defined as any person who regularly buys puppies in the hope of selling them for profit. A person who buys puppies as an agent for a known individual is not necessarily a dealer.) No puppy should be sold or offered as a prize in a raffle or competition.

9 Prospective buyers of puppies should be screened for suitability and should be advised of the known characteristics of the Cairn Terrier as a breed with the need for grooming and exercise. Puppies should not be sold to homes where they will be on their own all day.

10 No puppy with any physical defect, or which shows any definite departure from the Standard, should be sold without the buyer being made fully aware of such defect or departure from the Standard and its possible consequences. Members should sell only animals which to the best of their knowledge are in good health at the time of the sale.

11 Each purchaser of a Cairn puppy should be provided, at the time of the sale, with a pedigree, diet sheet and information about training, worming and inoculation.

12 No puppy that is of unregistered, or partly unregistered, parentage should be sold without the buyer being made aware that he will be unable to register it on the Kennel Club breed register.

13 It should be impressed on buyers that they should contact the breeder in the event of any problem with the puppy. Breeders should make every effort to be of assistance in these circumstances.

14 Advertising by members should be as factual as possible. Misleading exaggeration or unfounded implications of superiority should not be used. Members should refrain from making unfair or untrue statements about the dogs or practices of others.

15 Officers or committee members of the Club are always ready to do their best to help members with any queries or problems.

The Cairn Terrier Relief Fund

This fund was established in March, 1969 at a meeting held by dedicated Cairn Terrier fanciers at Dursley, Gloucestershire.

The Fund's objectives include the provision of a humane service of rehabilitation for Cairn Terriers who have become destitute for diverse reasons. Most breeds these days have their Rescue Officers and their telephone numbers are listed by the R.S.P.C.A. and many police stations. The Fund provides this service either in the form of purchasing dogs which are in need of assistance, or by paying for boarding prior to placing the subject in a new home, or by any other way of helping the animal. The Fund is administered by officers appointed from all of the breed clubs, and a very wide geographical area is thereby covered. All the helpers work voluntarily for the good of the breed and the need for their services has increased over recent years for many more Cairns have required rehabilitation, common to the experience suffered by most other breeds. The Fund welcomes offers of help in the way of accommodation for destitute Cairns and such should be conveyed to the local area representative. A list of the Trustees involved is given below, the letters above each indicating the club represented.

For the C.T.C.
Mr J. Pollock, 2 West Donnington Street, Darvel, Ayrshire (0560) 20530

Miss S. Appleby, West View, Holywell Lane, Sunniside, Newcastle-upon-Tyne (091–488) 1035

For the C.T.A.
Mr N. Roskell, 7 Oaktree Avenue, Ingol, Preston (0772) 726322

Miss T. P. Browne, The Hawthornes, Newmans Lane, West Moors, Dorset (0202) 872090

For the S.C.T.C.
Miss C. H. Dixon (Chairman), The Sanctuary, Steeple Ashton, Trowbridge, Wilts (0380) 870337

Mr H. Price (Hon. Sec.), Rustlings, 1A Winterhill Way, Burpham, Guildford, Surrey (0483) 66643

For the M.C.T.C.
Mrs C. Roberts, 603 Littleworth Road, Rawnsley, Cannock, Staffs. (054) 385403

Mr B. Mears, 82 Beacon Road, Rolleston, Burton-on-Trent (0283) 814406

For the N.I.C.T.C.
Mrs W. Dean, 19 Terryhoogan Road, Scarva, Craigavon, Co. Armagh, N.I. (0762) 831458

Mr A. McCrum, 7 Rathblane, Antrim, N.I. (08494) 64664

For the S.W. & W. of E.C.T.C.
Mrs M. Bendall, Pengorse Cottage, Moorland Road, Indian Queens, St Columb, Cornwall (0726) 860798

Mrs J. Keech, Cobwebs, Hillesley, nr. Wotton-u-Edge, Gloucestershire (0453) 842054

NOTE: It is inevitable that the above list of names of the Trustees and/or their addresses will need revision from time to time. An up-to-date list as it affects your locality is always obtainable from your local breed club secretary.

Breed clubs around the world

While a few of the clubs listed deal specifically with Cairn Terriers, others cater for Terriers generally, most of them finding the Cairn strongly represented in their total membership. Where a brief history of individual activities has become available, this is given for interest.

AUSTRALIA

The Cairn Terrier Club of Victoria Mrs R. Heim, Box 38, Lancefield 3435, Victoria, Australia. This club was founded in 1945 and has now a membership of about 170 scattered from Perth in Western Australia to the Queensland area. The club publishes a quarterly bulletin/newsletter which provides the main link between the widely separated members. Many within a hundred miles of Melbourne meet regularly to discuss club and breed topics and to attend the shows. The club supports the R.S.P.C.A. Veterinary Faculty at Melbourne University with annual donations. About ninety per cent of the Cairns in Victoria are kept as pets. At most fixtures twelve is an average entry, with eighty-five attending at the annual championship show, so reports the former honorary secretary, Miss P. M. Russell.

The Cairn Terrier Club of New South Wales Miss M. Hill, 47 Abbotsford Road, Homebush 2140, New South Wales, Australia.

BELGIUM

Belgian Terrier Club Mr A. Demullier, Chausee du Clorbus, 107 B-7700 Mouscron, Belgium (Tel. 056/33.36.39). Includes Cairn Terriers.

CANADA

Cairn Terrier Club of Canada Mrs Linda E. Kettlewell, 'Linwell' 49 Roberts Crescent, Brampton, Ontario, Canada L6W IG9. The club came into its own in 1973 after an earlier start which had proved abortive. The early seventies saw a considerable increase in the Cairn Terrier's popularity in Canada and the club was re-activated due to the efforts of Roger and Audrey Bailey with a number of other enthusiasts. James G. McFarlane became president and a committee was appointed with a constitution and a code of ethics set up to protect the Cairn Terrier. With Mr McFarlane's death in 1983 Roger Bailey became president and he was succeeded in 1987 by Mrs Gloria (Chicki) Mair.

A newsletter was first published in 1975, and is now issued quarterly and it has proved a great encouragement to breed enthusiasts, especially to those in far-flung districts. A Rescue and Research body was set up in 1985 after a decade in which members had been requested to rescue Cairns who had been abandoned in animal shelters. Later, funds were allocated to veterinary colleges for research on diseases affecting short-legged Terriers. The club held its first speciality show in Toronto in June 1976, the late Alice Hogg judging, since which time there has always been a U.K. American or Canadian judge to officiate its shows. Two western speciality shows have been held, Winnipeg in 1982, Edmonton in 1985. 1986 saw a record breed entry with 95 Cairns at Niagara Falls, Ontario, with William McCulloch the judge. In 1987 Mrs Sally Ogle from Scotland was the judge. Plans are already in hand for the visit of popular Mr Frank Edwards who will judge the Eastern Speciality in 1988; then there is a western speciality being planned for 1988. Many of the club's top show specimens are Canadian bred for many generations and its officials liaise with other clubs worldwide.

DENMARK
Dansk Terrier Club Mr Are Nielsen, Søndersøvej 18, 3500 Varløse, Denmark (Tel. 02 48 42 88). Includes Cairn Terriers.

FINLAND
Cairn Terrier Club of Finland Mrs Anna Koskivaara, Käsikiventie 8, 00920 Helsinki.

FRANCE
Les Amateurs de Terriers d'Ecosse Mr Hiverneaux, 14 Rue Alienor d'Aquitaine 17650 St Denis d'Oleron. (Tel. 46–479415). President: Mrs A. Wawra, 1 Rue Beaujon-75008 Paris. This club was founded in 1936 and caters for Cairns, Scottish Terriers, West Highlands and Skyes, but not Border Terriers who were taken over one year before by the Airedale club. There are about 1600 members and Cairn people account for the majority percentage. In 1986 they had 615 Cairns born and over 1000 enquiries for stock. The breed is definitely on the increase in France it being a good 'utility' variety – size, easy care and super personality giving it high points. Mrs Parker-Tucker judged their championship show in 1986 with Frank Edwards the year before. Jack Watson judged them in June 1987 in Orleans.

GERMANY
Klub für Terrier e.V., Schöne Aussicht 9, 6092 Kelsterbach/Main, FRG, Germany. *Rassebetreuer* (Breed-carer): Robert L. Fischer, 4440 Rhein, Salinenstr., 150a/Tierpark, Rheine, W. Germany (Tel. 05971–4128).

HOLLAND
The Cairn Terrier Club of Holland Mrs L. E. Winning Reepmaker, Buurtweg 44, 6971 KM OEKEN (GEM. BRUMMEN). (Tel. 5757–415) Puppies: Mr Simona, Winterwijk. (Tel: 5430–20551).

NEW ZEALAND
Four clubs which cater for complete Terrier group including Cairns which are strongly represented.

Canterbury Combined Terrier Club Mrs J. Ferris, 74 Sylvan Street, Christ-church 2, South Island, N.Z.

Central Terrier Club Mrs P. Plummer, P.O. Box 181, Waikanae, North Island, N.Z.

Hawkes Bay Terrier Club Mr F. R. Logan, Loganholme, R.D.2, Hastings, North Island, N.Z.

The Terrier Club Mrs J. Parkinson, 152 Solar Road, Glen Eden, Auckland, North Island, N.Z.

NORWAY
Cairn Terrier Club of Norway Mr Knut Range, Sagmesterveien 19, 141 Trollansen.

SOUTH AFRICA
South African Short-legged Terrier Club Hon. Sec. Mr G. Steyn. Chairman: G. Stein: P.O. Box 853, Johannesburg 200, South Africa. (Tel. 315–1289 and 674–1471 respectively.) Cairns are not catered for independently, but the S-L.T.C. covers all the Scottish breeds and a number of Sealyhams and Skyes. It was founded in 1923 and has passed through some lean years, but has always been supported by Miss M. Brigg ('Pibroch'), Miss N. Hodgkins ('Rossie') and Mrs D. Leftwhich ('Rochfort'). Good specimens have been imported from 'Blencathra', 'Rustlebury', 'Felshott', 'Courtrai' and 'Uniquecottage'. The club's twenty-seventh annual championship show was judged in 1987 by Mr J. W. L. McKee. The membership varies between 150 and 200. It is a very active and dedicated body.

SWEDEN
Cairn Terrier Club of Sweden Mrs Catarina Köhler, Villa Asplund, PL2494-64-45, Kuicksund.

UNITED STATES OF AMERICA
The Cairn Terrier Club of America Mrs Karen Wilson, 7010 Davis Ford Road, Manassas, VA 22111.

Appendix 2

Registrations

The Kennel Club's headquarters is at: 1 Clarges Street, Piccadilly, London, W1Y 8AB. General Enquiries: 01–493 6651; Registration Enquiries: 01–493 2001; Telegraphic Address: 'Staghound London W1'. Its Patron is Her Majesty Queen Elizabeth II with HRH Prince Michael of Kent FIMI its President. The Club's chairman is Mr J. A. MacDougall, M.Chir., FRCS, FRCSE and Senior Executive and Secretary Maj. Gen. M. H. Sinnatt, CB. The committee is made up with many noted folk from the dog world.

The objects of the club are to exist mainly for the purpose of promoting the improvement of dogs, Dog Shows, Field Trials, Working Trials and Obedience Tests and its objects include the classification of breeds, the framing and enforcement of Kennel Club Rules, the awarding of Challenge, Champion and other Certificates, the registration of Associations, Clubs and Societies and the publication of an annual *Stud Book* and a monthly *Kennel Gazette*. Every breeder should make sure that his home-bred stock is registered at the Kennel Club and also insist that his colleague breeders do the same. By so doing, the breed's 'official' numerical strength is increased, and championship show managements will maintain, even improve, their support.

Cairn Terriers prove by their registration figures at the Kennel Club that in Britain the variety is among the most popular breeds in the Terrier Group. This is probably due to the dog's 'useful' small size, always an asset in a breed striving for the popularity stakes, coupled with an unspoilt character and an easy adaptability to domestic life. In the field, even the veriest tyro can provide his owner with a pleasant afternoon and with the added armament of a lovable and sympathetic nature, a high degree of intelligence and absolute loyalty to his master, it is small wonder the Cairn is in great demand. The breed is an old one with centuries of evolution to boast about. If a breed can get near to perfection the Cairn Terrier can. The big Championship shows, Cruft's especially, have popularised Cairns and the ringside at this major show is invariably six or more deep. Today the breed is known and appreciated in thousands of homes, strongly competitive in the exhibition world and reproducing itself true to type and quality.

The following are annual (January to December) registration total figures from 1919:

1919	1920	1921	1922	1923	1924	1925	1926	1927	1928	1929	1930
197	388	572	727	1006	1220	1502	1745	1986	2223	2312	2688

1931	1932	1933	1934	1935	1936	1937	1938	1939	1940	1941	1942
2399	2504	2769	2665	2905	2703	2567	2366	1402	481	534	822

1943	1944	1945	1946	1947	1948	1949	1950	1951	1952	1953	1954
1302	1768	2248	2629	3645	3131	3296	2896	2756	2269	2391	2341

1955	1956	1957	1958	1959	1960	1961	1962	1963	1964	1965	1966
2513	2643	2628	2759	2969	3078	3426	3375	3284	3206	3642	3354

1967	1968	1969	1970	1971	1972	1973	1974	1975	1976	1977	1978
3670	3862	4001	3860	3163	3493	3336	3358	2864	*1345	* 945	*2442

1979	1980	1981	1982	1983	1984	1985	1986	1987 (to 31 March)
3162	3141	2571	2384	2411	2427	2509	2322	557

*Active Registration figures only. No figures recorded for the Basic Register.

Appendix 3

Selected Bibliography

Few of the following books deal purely and simply with the Cairn Terrier, while many are concerned with his ancestry and the development of his roots and the complexities of his eventual evolvement to show status. A number of sporting titles have been included as these contain material contributing to a serious study of this breed.

ASH, E. C.: *Dogs: Their History and Development*, London, 1927
    Practical Dog Book, London, 1927
    The Cairn Terrier, London, 1936
ATKINSON, E. S.: *Greyfriars Bobby*, N.Y., c1912
    Greyfriars Bobby, Sydney, 1949
BAIRACLI-LEVY, Juliette de: *The Complete Herbal Handbook for the Dog, in Health and Sickness*, London, 1952 and later eds.
BARTON, F. T.: *Dogs: Their Selection, Breeding and Keeping*, London, 1910
BELL, T.: *A History of British Quadrupeds*, London, 1837
BEYNON, J. W. H.: *The Popular Cairn Terrier*, London, 1929
    ——and FISHER, Alex: *The Cairn Terrier*, London, 1962
CASPERSZ, T. W. L. and D. S.: *Cairn Terrier Records*, Henley-on-Thames, 1932 and Supplements
    ——, D. S.: *The Scottish Terrier, Redhill, 1951*
    ——, T. W. L.: *The Cairn Terrier Handbook*, Redhill, 1957
CHAUNDLER, C.: *The Odd Ones*, London, 1941
DALZIEL, H.: *British Dogs*, London, 1879–80
DANIEL, Rev. W. B.: *Rural Sports*, London, 1801
DENNIS, D. M. and OWEN, C.: *The West Highland White Terrier* 1967 and later eds.
DRURY, W. D.: *British Dogs*, London, 1901–3
'An Expert': *Dog Lover's Companion*, London, c1937
FIORONE, F.: *The Encyclopaedia of the Dog*, London, 1973
GABRIEL, D.: *The Scottish Terrier*, London, 1928
GORDON, John F.: *The Dandie Dinmont Terrier*, London, 1959
GRAY, D. J. T.: *The Dogs of Scotland*, 1887–91, Dundee
GROSS, A.: *Das Bilderbuch der Hunde*, Hannover, 1967 (in German)
HAMILTON, F. (Ed.): *The World Encyclopaedia of Dogs*, London, 1971
HEATLEY, G. S.: *Our Dogs and Their Diseases*,
HUTTON, H.: *The True Story of Greyfriars Bobby*, Edinburgh, 1902
HUBBARD, C. L. B.: *Dogs in Britain*, Ponterwyd, 1946
    Working Dogs of the World, Ponterwyd, 1949
    The Literature of British Dogs, Ponterwyd, 1949
    The Complete Dog Breeders' Manual, London, 1954

Hutchinson's Popular & Illustrated Dog Encyclopaedia, London, 1935
JOHNS, R.: *Our Friend the Cairn*, London, 1932
— and NAYLOR, L. E.: *Dogs for Profit*, 1937
KNOWLES, G. W.: *The Book of Dogs*, London, 1920
LANE, C. H.: *Dog Shows and Doggy People*, London, 1902
LEE, Rawdon B.: *Modern Dogs* (Terriers), London, 1896
LANDSEER, Sir Edwin: *The Works of Sir Edwin Landseer*, London, 1875
LEIGHTON, R.: *The New Book of the Dog*, London, 1907
The Complete Book of the Dog, London, 1922
McCANDLISH, W. L.: *The Scottish Terrier*, 1906 from *Dogs: By Well Known Authorities*
MAXTEE, J.: *Scotch and Irish Terriers*, London, 1909
MEYRICK, J.: *House Dogs and Sporting Dogs*, London, 1861
MILES, H. D. (Ed.): *The Book of Field Sports*, London, 1860
MORRIS, T. O.: *Dogs and Their Doings*, London, 1869
PEERS, Graham, S. *Cairn '85*, Berkeley, 1985. Ed. J. Radford. Donated 1985 to
S.W.& W. of E.C.T.C.
PENN-BULL, Betty: *The Kennelgarth Scottish Terrier Book*, Hindhead, 1983
ROBERTSON, J.: *Historical Sketches of the Scottish Terrier*, Leeds, 1900
ROGERS, B.: *Cairns and Sealyham Terriers*, N.Y., 1922
Kennel Aristocrats, 1915–16, London, 1915
ROSS, F. M.: *The Cairn Terrier*, Manchester n.d. (?1924)
ROSS, Bishop of (John Lesley) *Scotland, Historie of from 1436–1561*, Edinburgh, 1830
SCHNEIDER-LEYER, Dr E.: *Dogs of the World*, London, 1964–70
SERRELL, Alys F.: *With Hound and Terrier in the Field*, Edinburgh, 1904
SHAW, Vero K.: *The Illustrated Book of the Dog*, London, 1879–81
SMALL, Hazel: *Cairns in Particular*, Tiverton, 1986 (Relief Fund Publication)
SMITH, A. Croxton: *Everyman's Book of the Dog*, London, 1909
The Kennel (Monthly Magazine), London, 1910–12
About Our Dogs, London, 1931
Hounds and Dogs, London, 1932
STABLES, A. C.: *The Livestock Journal*, 1879
Our Friend the Dog, London, 1879
Dog Owners' Kennel Companion and Referee, London, 1890
'STONEHENGE' – see J. H. Walsh
TURNER, J. S.: *The Kennel Encyclopaedia*, London, 1907
'*The Supplement*' Bulletin edited by Mrs T. Simpson Shaw in the beginning of the
present century
VESEY FITZGERALD, B.: *The Book of the Dog*, London, 1948
WALSH, J. H.: *The Dogs of the British Islands*, London, 1867
WATSON, J.: *The Dog Book*, London, 1906
WEBB, H.: *Book of Dogs: Their Points, Whims, Instincts and Peculiarities*, 1872
WEST, S.: *The Book of Dogs*, Tonbridge, 1935
WHITEHEAD, H. F.: *Cairn Terriers*, London, 1959
WOODWARD, J.: *The Cairn Terrier*, London, n.d.
YOUATT, W.: *The Dog*, London, 1845

The breed student is directed also to the numerous Year Books and Bulletins issued over the years by specialist breed clubs and associations involved with the Cairn Terrier. From these books much is to be gleaned.

Appendix 4

The Cairn Terrier in America

The earliest importation of an 'authenticated' Cairn Terrier from Britain into the United States of America is attributed to Mrs Harriet L. Price of the 'Robinscroft' kennels, Riverside, Connecticut in the autumn of 1913, just two years after the breed had been made official in Britain. This was a breeding pair purchased from Mrs Noney Fleming of the famous 'Out of the West' kennels following an introduction by Lady Charles Bentinck. Their names were 'Sandy Peter Out of the West' and 'Loch Scolter's Podge'. The former was a son of the then famous (in Britain) 'Loch Scolter' who was bred by Mrs Fleming and did in fact get two American champions in 'Froach Gail' and 'Bagpipes'. Mrs Price's interest in the breed had been stirred by a picture published in a London fashion journal – prior to that no one had ever heard of a Cairn. With her import and subsequent interest she became the breed founder in America, doing for the States much as Mrs Alastair Campbell had done for the breed in Britain. She entered her new breed in the Miscellaneous class at Danbury, Connecticut in October, 1913. The Miscellaneous class was a stand-by class scheduled to receive scarce and unusual breeds about which not much was known. *The Modern Dog Encyclopaedia*, 1949 published by Stackpole of Harrisburg, Pennsylvania, edited by Henry P. Davis, states that she exhibited both her imports and won first with the dog and third with the bitch. Danbury was pleased with the interest shown and actually scheduled the Cairn Terrier as a breed class for the following year. This was the first time the Cairn had its own breed class in America. Later in the same year Mrs Price entered at the noted Westminster show and won third prize with her dog 'Peter' in a highly competitive Miscellaneous class of seventeen.

Mrs Price bred her first litter in 1914. It was whelped 29 Sept 1914 and included 'Peter Piper', 'Miss Prim' and 'Prometheus' who was to become a champion in 1921 and had the honour of campaigning his breed alongside his enthusiastic owner for 14 years until his death in 1928. His sire, 'Sandy Peter Out of the West' was the first Cairn to enter his breed Register at the American Kennel Club, but to Mrs H. W. Warden of Philadelphia went the signal honour of having her 'Lorne Spirag' registered as America's first home-bred Cairn. This Cairn was sired by 'Lorne Padraig' out of 'Lorne Feorag', whelped 7 May 1914.

A big event was the noted Ladies Kennel Association show of 3 and 4 June

1915 where the Cairn had classification at the Mineola, New York venue. This had the great attraction of having Mr Holland Buckley on the woolsack.

Progress on the breed register proved quite slow in the next few years, although in 1917 when the Cairn Terrier Club of America was embraced by the American Kennel Club it did much for Cairns and membership. The original officers were as follows: President: Mrs Payne Whitney ('Greentree'); vice-president: William R. Wanamaker, secretary: Mrs Byron Rogers ('Misty Isles') and treasurer: Mrs H. F. Price ('Robinscroft'). From this date great progress was made, halted to a degree during the great world slump of the thirties. Today the breed excels in numbers, quality and in its judges. The breed has done great things in the Obedience world too. Long may such progress continue. One can be proud of the fact that the Cairn Terrier has never been over-commercialised. Once that happens it usually signals the death-knell of a breed, starting off with the ruination of type and soundness and ending with the debilitation of temperament.

American Breed Standard of the Cairn Terrier

Reproduced by kind permission of the American Kennel Club.

General appearance That of an active, game, hardy, small working terrier of the short-legged class; very free in its movements, strongly but not heavily built, standing well forward on its forelegs, deep in the ribs, well coupled with strong hindquarters and presenting a well-proportioned build with a medium length of back, having a hard, weather-resisting coat; head shorter and wider than any other terrier and well furnished with hair giving a general foxy expression.

Head
Skull – Broad in proportion to length with a decided stop and well furnished with hair on the top of the head, which may be somewhat softer than the body coat. *Muzzle* – Strong but not too long or heavy. *Teeth* – Large, mouth neither overshot nor undershot. *Nose* – Black. *Eyes* – Set wide apart, rather sunken, with shaggy eyebrows, medium in size, hazel or dark hazel in colour, depending on body colour, with a keen terrier expression. *Ears* – Small, pointed, well carried erectly, set wide apart on the side of the head. Free from long hairs.

Tail In proportion to head, well furnished with hair but not feathery. Carried gaily but must not curl over back. Set on at back level.

Body Well-muscled, strong, active body with well-sprung, deep ribs, coupled to strong hindquarters, with a level back of medium length, giving an impression of strength and activity without heaviness.

Shoulders, Legs and Feet A sloping shoulder, medium length of leg, good but not too heavy bone; forelegs should not be out at elbows, and be perfectly straight, but forefeet may be slightly turned out. Forefeet larger than hind feet. Legs must be covered with hard hair. Pads should be thick and strong and dog should stand well up on its feet.

Coat Hard and weather-resistant. Must be double-coated with profuse harsh outer coat and short, soft, close furry undercoat.

Colour May be of any colour except white. Dark ears, muzzle and tail tip are desirable.

Ideal size Involves the weight, the height at the withers and the length of body. Weight for bitches, 13 pounds; for dogs, 14 pounds. Height at the withers – bitches, $9\frac{1}{2}$ inches; dogs, 10 inches. Length of body from $14\frac{1}{4}$ to 15 inches from the front of the chest to back of hindquarters. The dog must be of balanced proportions and appear neither leggy nor too low to ground; and neither too short nor too long in body. Weight and measurements are for matured dogs at two years of age. Older dogs may weigh slightly in excess and growing dogs may be under these weights and measurements.

Condition Dogs should be shown in good hard flesh, well-muscled and neither too far or thin. Should be in full good coat with plenty of head furnishings, be clean, combed, brushed and tidied up on ears, tail, feet and general outline. Should move freely and easily on a loose lead, should not cringe on being handled, should stand up on their toes and show with marked terrier characteristics.

FAULTS
1. Skull – Too narrow in skull.
2. Muzzle – Too long and heavy a foreface; mouth overshot or undershot.
3. Eyes – Too large, prominent, yellow, and ringed are all objectionable.
4. Ears – Too large, round at points, set too close together, set too high on the head; heavily covered with hair.
5. Legs and Feet – Too light or too heavy bone. Crooked forelegs or out at elbow. Thin, ferrety feet; feet let down on the heel or too open and spread. Too high or too low on the leg.
6. Body – Too short back and compact a body, hampering quickness of movement and turning ability. Too long, weedy and snaky a body, giving an impression of weakness. Tail set on too low. Back not level.
7. Coat – Open coats, blousy coats, too short or dead coats, lack of sufficient undercoat, lack of head furnishings, lack of hard hair on the legs. Silkiness or curliness. A slight wave permissible.
8. Nose – Flesh or light-coloured nose.
9. Colour – White on chest, feet or other parts of body.

© American Kennel Club *Approved May 10, 1938*

The following shows the annual (January to December) registration total figures for Cairn Terriers at the American Kennel Club, from 1913:

1913	1914	1915	1916	1917	1918	1919	1920	1921	1922	1923	1924
1	5	nil	8	32	34	70	91	59	67	107	120

1925	1926	1927	1928	1929	1930	1931	1932	1933	1934	1935	1936
124	208	217	181	205	348	347	311	344	431	562	580

1937	1938	1939	1940	1941	1942	1943	1944	1945	1946	1947	1948
556	498	419	427	411	341	252	170	340	426	516	392

1949	1950	1951	1952	1953	1954	1955	1956	1957	1958	1959	1960
482	535	501	585	632	632	622	752	776	872	929	982

1961	1962	1963	1964	1965	1966	1967	1968	1969	1970	1971	1972
1076	1270	1401	1899	2369	2883	3968	4532	5677	6698	7738	7753

1973	1974	1975	1976	1977	1978	1979	1980	1981	1982	1983	1984
7497	7339	6365	6432	6359	6369	6262	6561	6346	6108	6154	5892

1985	1986
5807	6030

In Conclusion . . .

The following are some pithy extracts from the verses written by Dr Gordon Stables, R.N., in *The Livestock Journal*, 31 January, 1879 when he was touring the Highlands in his caravan on a fact-finding tour. So well do his words 'fit' the Cairn Terrier, known then as the Highland Terrier, that they are worthy of record in this book:

I ken the Terrier o' the North,
    I ken the towsy tyke –

Ye'll search frae Tweed to Sussex'
                      shore,
    But never find his like.

He'll face a foumart, draw a brock,
    Kill rats and whitteritts by the
                      score,
He'll bang tod-lowrie frae his hole,
    Or slay him at his door.

He'll range for days and ne'r be
                      tired,
    O'er mountain, Moor and fell;
Fair play, I'll back the brave wee
                      chap
    To fecht the de'il himsel'.

And yet beneath his rugged coat,
    A heart beats warm and true,
He'll help to herd the sheep and
                      kye,
    And mind the lammies too.

Then see him at the ingle side,
    Wi' bairnies round him laughin',
Was ever dog sae pleased as he,
    Sae fond o' fun and daffin'?

fourmart = polecat
brock = badger
tod-lowrie = fox
whitteritt = weasel

Published in Robert Leighton's *New Book of the Dog*, 1907

Index